I0820540

UNOFFICIAL & UNAUTHORISED

YOU BELONG WITH BRIE

BFF FOREVER

UNOFFICIAL & UNAUTHORISED

YOU BELONG WITH BRIE

60 Recipes Inspired by ★ Taylor Swift ★

hamlyn

First published in Great Britain
in 2025 by Hamlyn, an imprint of
Octopus Publishing Group Ltd
Carmelite House
50 Victoria Embankment
London EC4Y 0DZ
www.octopusbooks.co.uk
www.octopusbooksusa.com

An Hachette UK Company
www.hachette.co.uk

The authorized representative in the EEA is Hachette Ireland, 8 Castlecourt Centre, Dublin 15, D15 XTP3, Ireland (email: info@hbgi.ie)

Distributed in the US by
Hachette Book Group
1290 Avenue of the Americas,
4th and 5th Floors
New York, NY 10104

Distributed in Canada by
Canadian Manda Group
664 Annette St., Toronto,
Ontario, Canada M6S 2C8

ISBN: 978-0-600-63968-8
eISBN: 978-0-600-63969-5

A CIP catalogue record for this book is available from the British Library.

Printed and bound in China.

10 9 8 7 6 5 4 3 2 1

Commissioning Editor: Isabel Jessop
Production Manager: Caroline Alberti

With thanks to Swiftie consultants Charlotte, Chris, Isobel, Jeannie, Louisa, Madeleine and Xavia

Sources: p.12, *Women's Health* 3 November 2008; p.88 *TIME* 24 April 2019; p.92 *Rolling Stone* 24 July 2020; p.97 @taylorswift 10 April 2020 and @austinkingsleyswift 13 December 2018; p.129 *Billboard* 15 May 2015

Some of this material has previously appeared in other Hamlyn All Colour Cookbooks.

★ CONTENTS ★

INTRODUCTION	7
BREAKFAST	8
LUNCH	24
DINNER	56
DESSERT	86
DRINKS	118
INDEX	142

COOKING NOTES

Standard level spoon measurements are used in all recipes.

1 tablespoon = one 15 ml spoon

1 teaspoon = one 5 ml spoon

Both imperial and metric measurements have been given in all recipes. Use one set of measurements only and not a mixture of both.

Eggs should be medium unless otherwise stated. The Department of Health advises that eggs should not be consumed raw. This book contains dishes made with raw or lightly cooked eggs. It is prudent for more vulnerable people such as pregnant and nursing mothers, invalids, the elderly, babies and young children to avoid uncooked or lightly cooked dishes made with eggs. Once prepared these dishes should be kept refrigerated and used promptly.

Milk should be full fat unless otherwise stated.

Fresh herbs should be used unless otherwise stated. If unavailable use dried herbs as an alternative but halve the quantities stated.

Ovens should be preheated to the specific temperature – if using a fan-assisted oven, follow manufacturer's instructions for adjusting the time and the temperature.

Pepper should be freshly ground black pepper unless otherwise stated.

This book includes dishes made with nuts and nut derivatives. It is advisable for those with known allergic reactions to nuts and nut derivatives and those who may be potentially vulnerable to these allergies, such as pregnant and nursing mothers, the elderly, babies and children, to avoid dishes made with nuts and nut oils. It is also prudent to check the labels of pre-prepared ingredients for the possible inclusion of nut derivatives.

Vegetarians should look for the 'V' symbol on a cheese to ensure it is made with vegetarian rennet.

INTRODUCTION

Welcome to your culinary era – it's been waiting for you! You're about to become a star performer in your own kitchen thanks to these Taylor Swift-themed recipes! Inspired by Taylor's lyrics, life and eras, whether you're baking up a storm during a Cruel Summer or You Need to Calm Down over what to make for dinner, there's something inside to make every mealtime a hit. Fun facts about Taylor's world are also sprinkled throughout to add some extra showstopping sparkle!

Each recipe has simple, step-by-step instructions to follow with no need for special equipment. There are hot and cold ideas for Breakfast, Lunch, Dinner and Dessert, along with a Drinks section that includes cocktails and non-alcoholic 'mocktails' that never go out of style. There's also some Blank Space at the end of the book for your own notes. Before you know it, you'll be eating and drinking like a megastar!

XOXO

BREAKFAST

SHAKSHUKA IT OFF

SERVES 2 | PREP: 10mins | COOKING TIME: 25–35mins

If you've stayed out too late, this is the breakfast to help you feel alright again! These Moroccan baked eggs are warmly spiced, filling without being heavy, and ready in minutes. If you don't have cherry tomatoes, substitute these with a can of chopped tomatoes. Now you're ready to shake, shake, shakshuka it off and start the day!

★ FUN FACT ★

The music video for 'Shake It Off' was directed by director Mark Romanek, who previously created videos with Michael Jackson, David Bowie, Lenny Kravitz and Madonna!

SHAKSHUKA IT OFF

★ INGREDIENTS ★

½ tablespoon olive oil
½ onion, chopped
1 garlic clove, sliced
½ teaspoon ras el hanout
pinch of ground cinnamon
½ teaspoon ground coriander
400g (13oz) cherry tomatoes
2 tablespoons chopped coriander
4 eggs
salt and pepper
crusty bread or flatbread, to serve

★ METHOD ★

1. Heat the oil in a frying pan, add the onion and garlic and cook for 6–7 minutes until softened and lightly golden. Stir in the three different spices and cook, stirring, for a further minute.
2. Add the cherry tomatoes and season well with salt and pepper, then simmer gently for 8–10 minutes.
3. Make four wells in the tomato mixture with a spoon. Break an egg into each well, taking care to keep the yolk intact. Scatter over 1 tablespoon of the coriander.
4. Bake in a preheated oven, 220°C (425°F), Gas Mark 7, for 8–10 minutes until the egg whites are set but the yolks are still slightly runny. Cook for a further 2–3 minutes if you prefer the eggs to be cooked through. Garnish with the remaining coriander.
5. Serve with lightly toasted crusty bread or flatbread.

CHRISTMAS TREE FARM PASTRIES

SERVES 4 | PREP: 10mins (plus 30mins soaking time for wooden skewers)

COOKING TIME: 10–15mins

They say 'write about what you know' which is why 'Christmas Tree Farm' isn't just Taylor's first seasonal song – it's a childhood memory come to life. Taylor grew up on Pine Ridge Farm, Wyomissing which is a real-life Christmas tree farm! Now you can experience the magic of Christmas at any time of year with these tree-inspired pastries!

★ QUOTE ★

"I know that a Christmas tree farm in Pennsylvania is about the most random place for a country singer to come from, but I had an awesome childhood."

CHRISTMAS TREE FARM PASTRIES

★ INGREDIENTS ★

320g (11oz) chilled ready-rolled puff pastry sheet

3–4 tablespoons Nutella or chocolate spread

beaten egg, for brushing

icing sugar, for dusting

wooden skewers, pre-soaked in cold water

★ METHOD ★

1. Line a large baking sheet with nonstick baking paper.
2. Unroll the pastry and cut off a 5cm (2 inch) wide strip from the short end. From this strip, use a star-shaped cutter to cut out six stars and set aside.
3. Cut the remaining pastry in half widthways to make 2 rectangles. Spread the Nutella or chocolate spread evenly over one of the pastry rectangles. Lay the other rectangle over the top and cut the pastry into four strips about 2.5cm (1 inch) thick.
4. Thread each pastry strip onto a wooden skewer, making 3–4 zig-zag folds to create a triangle, or Christmas tree, shape. Leave space between the folds to give the pastry room to expand as it bakes. Top each skewer with one of the pastry stars.
5. Brush with a beaten egg and place each skewer on the prepared baking sheet. Bake in a preheated oven, 200°C (400°F), Gas Mark 6, for 10–15 minutes until golden and puffed. Serve warm, dusted with icing sugar.

GUILTY AS CINAMMON ROLLS

SERVES 4 | PREP: 10mins | COOKING TIME: 15–20mins

There's nothing tortured about these cinnamon rolls, which couldn't be easier to make. In fact, they're so delicious, you'll be writing 'mine' on a label to make sure nobody steals them away. And if they do, just watch out for anyone who looks as guilty as sin …

★ FUN FACT ★

Taylor attended the 2025 Grammy Awards ceremony with a T pendant on a chain hanging over her thigh. She may not have won an award that night, but she was definitely the most on brand attendee!

GUILTY AS CINAMMON ROLLS

★ INGREDIENTS ★

4 tablespoons softened butter, plus extra for greasing

250g (8oz) can croissant dough

6 tablespoons soft brown sugar

3 teaspoons ground cinnamon

75g (3oz) pecan nuts, roughly chopped (optional)

2 tablespoons icing sugar, for dusting

★ METHOD ★

1. Lightly grease 2 baking sheets.
2. Unroll the croissant dough on a chopping board. Place the butter, sugar and cinnamon in a bowl and beat well with a wooden spoon until soft and well blended.
3. Spread the cinnamon butter evenly over the croissant dough, right to the edges. Sprinkle over the chopped pecans, if using, then tightly roll up the dough.
4. Cut the log into 4 thick pinwheels and place well apart on the prepared baking sheets. Bake in a preheated oven, 200°C (400°F), Gas Mark 6, for 15–20 minutes until well risen and golden. Serve warm, dusted with icing sugar.

MIDNIGHT MUFFINS

SERVES 12 | PREP: 15mins | COOKING TIME: 20mins

Within three hours of the *Midnights* album being released at midnight on October 21, 2022, the '3am Edition' arrived, with seven extra tracks that created a 20-song soundscape of pop perfection.

Each one of these Midnight Muffins will set you up for a dreamy day – and are so easy to make we guarantee there are no nightmares ahead. You don't even need to be up at midnight to make them! (But if you are, you know what you should be listening to!)

★ INGREDIENTS ★

275g (9oz) self-raising flour
2 teaspoons baking powder
100g (3½ oz) caster sugar
250g (8oz) fresh blueberries
2 eggs, beaten
50g (2oz) slightly salted butter, melted
200ml (7fl oz) milk
2 teaspoons vanilla extract

★ METHOD ★

1. Mix together the flour, baking powder and caster sugar in a bowl. Stir in the blueberries.
2. Beat together the eggs, melted butter, milk and vanilla in a jug. Add to the dry ingredients and stir together using a large metal spoon until just combined.
3. Divide the mixture evenly between paper muffin cases arranged in a 12-hole muffin tray. Bake in a preheated oven, 200°C (400°F), Gas Mark 6, for about 20 minutes until well risen and just firm to the touch.
4. Transfer to a wire rack. Serve warm or cold.

TOLER-OAT IT GRANOLA

SERVES 4 | PREP: 10mins, plus cooling

COOKING TIME: 20–25mins

With its winning combination of honey, nuts and dried fruit, once you've made this recipe, you'll never have to tolerate ready-made granola again. It's also easily adaptable to include whatever combination of dried fruit and nuts you prefer, so take inspiration from your store cupboard or your own breakfast preferences.

TOLER-OAT IT GRANOLA

★ INGREDIENTS ★

5 tablespoons clear honey

2 tablespoons sunflower oil

250g (8oz) porridge oats

50g (2oz) hazelnuts, roughly chopped

50g (2oz) blanched almonds, roughly chopped

50g (2oz) dried cranberries

50g (2oz) dried blueberries

★ METHOD ★

1. Heat the honey and oil together gently in a small saucepan.
2. Mix the oats and nuts together thoroughly in a large bowl. Pour over the warm honey mixture and stir well to combine.
3. Spread the mixture over a large nonstick baking sheet. Bake in a preheated oven, 150°C (300°F), Gas Mark 2, for 20–25 minutes, stirring once, until golden.
4. Leave the granola to cool, then stir in the dried berries. Serve with skimmed milk or low-fat bio yogurt and fresh fruit. Any remaining granola can be stored in an airtight container.

★ FUN FACT ★

The *Evermore* track, 'Tolerate It' was inspired by the 1938 gothic novel, *Rebecca*. Written by Daphne du Maurier, it tells the story of a mysterious widower, his manipulative housekeeper and the naïve young woman who becomes his second wife … at her own risk. Why not make like Taylor and check it out?

CHERRY LIPS BREAKFAST SMOOTHIE

SERVES 2 | PREP: 10mins

This silky smoothie is packed with antioxidant-rich blueberries and cherries to ensure your energy levels don't go down in flames before its time for lunch! If you like your smoothie a little more liquid, add a splash of apple juice to loosen the mixture as you blend. Whatever consistency you prefer, this tastes so good, it's going to leave you breathless!

CHERRY LIPS BREAKFAST SMOOTHIE

★ INGREDIENTS ★

100g (3½ oz) blueberries

200g (7oz) cherries, plus 2 reserved for decorating

1 tablespoon cashew nuts

1 tablespoon rolled oats

1 tablespoon cocoa nibs, plus extra to sprinkle

300 ml (½ pint) milk

★ METHOD ★

1. Juice the blueberries. Stone the cherries.
2. Transfer the blueberry juice and cherries to a food processor or blender. Add the cocoa nibs, cashew nuts, rolled oats and milk, and blitz until smooth.
3. Pour the smoothie into 2 glasses, sprinkle with some extra cocoa nibs and top with a cherry. Serve immediately.

★ FUN FACT ★

Taylor has had a long-standing love affair with red lipstick, but on the Eras Tour, it was the deep, blue-based red of Pat McGrath Labs' LiquiLust Legendary Wear Matte Lipstick in shade Elson 4 that hit the spot!

OUT OF THE WOODS BIRCHER MUESLI

SERVES 4 | PREP: 10mins

It's time to wrap up our breakfast selection, but you aren't 'oat' of the woods yet, Swifties! Coming in strong as an encore is this delicious Bircher muesli, or overnight oats, recipe. Once you've perfected the basic recipe, you can release a version of your own! Experiment with any topping you enjoy such as dried banana chips or cranberries, freshly sliced soft fruit or apple slices. You can also use all milk or all apple juice as the soaking liquid to change the flavour profile. Enjoy!

OUT OF THE WOODS BIRCHER MUESLI

★ INGREDIENTS ★

400g (13oz) fruit and nut muesli

2 dessert apples, peeled and coarsely grated

300ml (½ pint) semi-skimmed milk, heated

140ml (¼ pint) apple juice

250g (8oz) Greek yogurt

2 teaspoons golden linseeds (optional)

clear honey

★ METHOD ★

1. Place the muesli in a bowl and pour over the hot milk and apple juice. Stir well to combine and leave to soak for 15–20 minutes. If you have time, leave the oats to soak overnight in the fridge.
2. Divide the soaked muesli into serving bowls and spoon the yogurt on top of each one. Scatter over the linseeds, if using, and serve drizzled with some clear honey.

BFF FOREVER

LUNCH

YOU BELONG WITH BRIE

SERVES 4 | PREP: 20mins | COOKING TIME: 15mins

If you love having people over for lunch but don't want to spend ages in the kitchen, this is the dish for you! It looks impressive but only takes minutes to prepare, making it what you've been looking for the whole time. The cheese will be VERY hot after baking so don't be too fearless with those first few dips!

YOU BELONG WITH BRIE

★ INGREDIENTS ★

300g (10oz) whole baby Brie or Camembert

25g (1oz) pecan nuts

3 tablespoons maple syrup

3 tablespoons soft brown sugar

thyme sprigs

crusty bread, to serve

★ METHOD ★

1. Remove any plastic packaging from the cheese and return it to its wooden box. Place on a baking sheet and cook in a preheated oven, 200°C (400°F), Gas Mark 6, for 15 minutes.
2. Meanwhile, toast the pecans in a small frying pan for 3–5 minutes until lightly browned, then set aside. Put the maple syrup and sugar in a small saucepan and bring to the boil. Cook for 1 minute until foamy.
3. Take the cheese from the oven and cut a small cross in the centre. Drizzle over the maple syrup, scatter with the pecans and thyme and serve with plenty of crusty bread.

SHAWARMA IS MY BOYFRIEND

SERVES 4 | PREP: 5mins | COOKING TIME: 12–15mins

Keep your conscience clean by vibing with this healthy, veggie-packed lunch instead of ordering take-out. Karma will thank you! Experiment with the spices and seasoning to find your perfect match. Mixing chopped fresh mint leaves into Greek yogurt also makes a cooling alternative to the cream cheese.

★ FUN FACT ★

Karma is defined as experiencing good or bad luck as a result of your own actions. It's a relaxing thought if you've been keeping your side of the street clean, right? *stares in Taylor*

★ INGREDIENTS ★

4 boneless, skinless chicken breasts, cut into long thin slices

4 courgettes, cut into long thin slices

1 red pepper, cored, deseeded, quartered

1 yellow pepper, cored, deseeded, quartered

4 tablespoons olive oil

2 garlic cloves, finely chopped

4 teaspoons sun-dried tomato paste

2 teaspoons shawarma spice mix or garam masala

4 large soft flour tortillas

200g (7oz) cream cheese with garlic and herbs

3 tomatoes, sliced

salt and pepper

★ METHOD ★

1. Arrange the chicken breasts, courgettes and peppers in a single layer on a foil-lined grill rack or baking sheet.
2. Mix the oil, garlic, tomato paste, spice mix (or garam masala) and seasoning together and spoon over the chicken and vegetables. Grill for 12–15 minutes, turning everything once, until the vegetables are softened and browned and the chicken is cooked through.
3. Move the chicken to a separate plate or cutting board and let it rest for 5–10 minutes. Cut it into strips.
4. Warm the tortillas according to the instructions on the packet, then spread with the cream cheese. Cut the peppers into strips, peeling if liked. Divide the chicken and vegetables between the tortillas, add slices of tomato, then roll up tightly and cut in half. Serve warm.

ARE YOU BREADY FOR IT?

SERVES 4: PREP: 10mins, plus standing

COOKING TIME: 10mins

When is a salad more than a salad? When it's a panzanella! This Tuscan salad is steeped in robust flavours which will haunt your dreams in the middle of the night (in the best possible way). Are you ready for it?

★ FUN FACT ★

In 'Are You Ready For It?' Taylor references Richard Burton and Elizabeth Taylor. These acting co-stars had a famously tumultuous romantic history, marrying and divorcing twice, and creating headlines around the world with their fiery relationship dramas.

★ INGREDIENTS ★

2 red peppers, deseeded and sliced

3 tablespoons olive oil

650g (1lb 5oz) tomatoes, skinned, cored and chopped

1 red onion, finely sliced

handful of green olives

1 tablespoon capers, rinsed

1 red chilli, deseeded and finely chopped

handful of basil leaves

2 tablespoons red wine vinegar

4 tablespoons olive oil

200g (7oz) bread, cubed and toasted

salt and black pepper

★ METHOD ★

1. Put the red peppers on a baking sheet, drizzle over half the olive oil and place in a preheated oven 200°C (400°F), Gas Mark 6 for 10 minutes, turning after 5 minutes. Leave to cool then remove the skin.
2. Leave to cool. Mix all the remaining ingredients, apart from the toasted bread cubes, in a large bowl and set aside for at least 20 minutes to allow the flavours to develop.
3. Add the red peppers to the bowl when cooled. Just before serving, add the toasted bread cubes and stir gently to distribute them through the salad.

DELI-CATE BLT SANDWICH

SERVES 1 | PREP: 20mins | COOKING TIME: 5mins

Is it cool that of all the sandwiches, the BLT is the one that nobody ever wants to share? The crispiness of the hot bacon is perfectly balanced by the chilled mayonnaise, lettuce and tomato, making it classic deli sandwich filling. Bacon has a reputation for being salty, so you can add slices of turkey to help temper this, or use a reduced salt version.

DELI-CATE BLT SANDWICH

★ INGREDIENTS ★

4 back bacon rashers
6 slices of wholemeal bread
1 tablespoon mayonnaise
2 tomatoes, sliced
4 Little Gem lettuce leaves
potato chips, to serve

★ METHOD ★

1. Cook the bacon under a preheated hot grill for about 5 minutes, turning once, until crisp.
2. Toast the bread slices on both sides.
3. Spread the mayonnaise over 2 slices of the toast. Arrange the tomato slices on top.
4. Cover with another slice of toast, and top with the lettuce and bacon. Place the remaining slices of toast on top.
5. Press the sandwich stacks down firmly and cut in half. Stick a cocktail stick flag through each sandwich to hold it all together. Serve with potato chips.

★ DID YOU KNOW? ★

The co-writer of 'Delicate', from *Reputation*, is Max Martin. He has collaborated on ten songs with Taylor, including 'Shake It Off' and 'Blank Space', and written hits for artists including Ariana Grande, Britney Spears and Post Malone.

FILO-ING 22 SPINACH AND FETA PIE

SERVES 6 | PREP: 20mins

COOKING TIME: ABOUT 1 HOUR

I don't know about you, but I'm feeling ready for something Mediterranean! This filo spinach and feta pie originates in Greece, where it is called Spanakopita. To keep it traditional, serve with a Greek salad and tzatziki, or Greek lemon potatoes and roasted vegetables. The pie is even more delicious as a cold leftover – why not try eating it for breakfast at midnight after you've been dancing with strangers?

FILO-ING 22 SPINACH AND FETA PIE

★ INGREDIENTS ★

750g (1½ lb) fresh spinach leaves
250g (8oz) feta cheese, crumbled
½ teaspoon dried chilli flakes
75g (3oz) Parmesan cheese, grated
50g (2oz) pine nuts, toasted
3 teaspoons dill, chopped
3 teaspoons tarragon, chopped
3 eggs, beaten
pinch of grated nutmeg
250g (8oz) filo pastry
5–8 tablespoons olive oil
1 tablespoon sesame seeds
salt and pepper

★ METHOD ★

1. Wash the spinach and wilt in a large saucepan over a low heat until soft. Drain well. Mix the feta into the spinach with the chilli flakes, Parmesan, pine nuts and herbs. Stir in the eggs, salt, pepper and nutmeg.
2. Unwrap the filo pastry and brush the top sheet with a little olive oil. Lay in the bottom of a lightly greased 20cm (8 inch) loose-bottomed cake tin with the edges overlapping the rim. Brush the next sheet of pastry and lay it in the opposite direction to cover the base. Repeat with 4–6 sheets, saving 4 sheets to make a lid.
3. Spoon the spinach mixture into the filo pastry shell, pushing it in with the back of the spoon until the filling is level.
4. Place one of the remaining sheets on top of the filling and brush with oil. Cut the remaining pastry sheets into squares. Brush with oil and place them on top of the spinach to form a star shape. Alternatively, lightly crumple or twist the sheets and arrange them on the top.
5. Drizzle the pie with oil, sprinkle with sesame seeds and bake in a preheated oven, 190°C (375°F), Gas Mark 5, for 50–60 minutes. Leave to cool before serving.

THIS IS WHY WE CAN'T HAVE NICE WINGS

SERVES 4 | PREP: 30mins | COOKING TIME: 25mins

Bring the heat with these spicy wings! They're ideal for nibbling on with your real friends while discussing all the latest "he said, she said" gossip! The longer you can leave the wings to marinate, the richer the flavour once they're cooked. The coleslaw can be made the night before, leaving you maximum time to listen to all the drama. Maybe we can have nice things?

★ FUN FACT ★

'This Is Why We Can't Have Nice Things' is believed by some to be a response to Kanye West's behaviour towards Taylor over the years, which began with his infamous stage invasion at the 2009 MTV VMAs.

THIS IS WHY WE CAN'T HAVE NICE WINGS

★ INGREDIENTS ★

FOR THE WINGS

2 tablespoons clear honey

5 tablespoons tomato ketchup

2 teaspoons English mustard

2 teaspoons Worcestershire sauce

½–1 teaspoon hot chilli sauce

2 tablespoons sunflower oil

1kg (2lb) chicken wings

FOR THE COLESLAW

4 tablespoons mayonnaise

2 tablespoons lemon juice

375g (12oz) white cabbage, finely shredded

1 small red onion, finely shredded

1 medium carrot, coarsely grated

1 tablespoon chopped parsley

Pepper

★ METHOD ★

1. Combine the honey, ketchup, mustard, Worcestershire sauce, chilli sauce and oil in a bowl. Add the chicken wings and mix well to coat.
2. Put the chicken wings on a large, foil-lined baking sheet and bake in a preheated oven, 200°C (400°F), Gas Mark 6, for 25 minutes, turning occasionally and brushing with any remaining sauce in the bowl, until cooked through.
3. Meanwhile, make the coleslaw. Mix all the ingredients in a large bowl and season with pepper. Serve the chicken wings and coleslaw together.

WHO'S AFRAID OF LITTLE OLD HALLOUMI?

SERVES 2 | PREP: 10mins | COOKING TIME: 25mins

These mini pizzas, or pizzettas, make a change from sandwiches for lunch, but can also be adapted to different sizes for serving at social gatherings or even Superbowl watch parties! Just make sure you create the 'border' on each pastry base and bake these first to crisp up. Taylor has said that 'Who's Afraid of Little Old Me?' is written as a response to those who criticize creatives. So don't be afraid to be a creative artist and customize these pizzettas how you like! You could experiment with adding different cheeses, veggies or sauces.

WHO'S AFRAID OF LITTLE OLD HALLOUMI?

★ INGREDIENTS ★

1 sheet of puff pastry, 25cm (10 inch) square

3 tablespoons green pesto

4 fresh figs, quartered

200g (7oz) halloumi cheese, thinly sliced

50g (2oz) pitted black olives, halved

2 tablespoons freshly grated Parmesan cheese

a few mint leaves, to garnish

salt and black pepper

1. Preheat a baking sheet large enough for a second sheet to sit on. Lay the pastry on the cold baking sheet and score a 1cm (½ inch) border around the edge. Prick the base (not the border) with a fork and spread over the pesto.
2. Arrange the figs, halloumi and olives on top of the pesto and scatter over the Parmesan.
3. Place the baking sheet containing the pizzettas on the preheated baking sheet (this will ensure the pastry is crispy) and bake in a preheated oven, 200°C (400°F), Gas Mark 6, for 10 minutes.
4. Reduce the temperature to 160°C (325°F), Gas Mark 3, and bake for a further 15 minutes until the base is crispy. Scatter the mint leaves over to garnish and serve with salad.

FRIENDSHIP FRIES

SERVES 4 | PREP: 30mins | COOKING TIME: 35–40mins

While these circular fries are delicious on their own, the homemade ketchup lifts them to new heights. Their shape resembles the friendship bracelets which became an integral aspect of The Eras Tour. The trend was believed to have stemmed from a lyric in 'You're on Your Own' from *Midnights* and before long, swapping hand-crafted beaded friendship bracelets with fellow fans in and around each stadium represented the love, solidarity and respect between Swifties. If you didn't leave one of Taylor's concerts with a friendship bracelet, were you even there!?

FRIENDSHIP FRIES

★ INGREDIENTS ★

FOR THE FRIES

750g (1½ lb) potatoes, scrubbed and cut into 1cm (½ inch) round slices

2 tablespoons olive oil

1 teaspoon paprika

salt and pepper

FOR THE KETCHUP

1 tablespoon olive oil

½ onion, sliced

1 teaspoon finely grated fresh root ginger

1 garlic clove, crushed

½ teaspoon ground coriander

1 tablespoon tomato purée

200g (7oz) cherry tomatoes

4 tablespoons white wine vinegar

2 tablespoons soft brown sugar

salt and pepper

★ METHOD ★

1. Toss the potato slices with 2 tablespoons of the oil, season with the paprika, salt and pepper and place on a large baking tray. Place in a preheated oven, 220°C (425°F), Gas Mark 7, for 25 minutes. Turn the fries and bake for a further 10–15 minutes until golden and cooked through.

2. To make the ketchup, heat the oil in a saucepan. Add the onion and cook for 10 minutes until softened. Add the ginger, garlic, coriander and tomato purée and cook for a further 2 minutes. Add the tomatoes, vinegar, sugar and a splash of water. Leave to simmer for 10 minutes. Whizz in a small food processor or blender to form a chunky ketchup. Season to taste and serve with the friendship fries.

YOU BELONG WITH BRIE

BEJEWELED RICE PILAF

SERVES 3-4 | PREP: 20mins

COOKING TIME 1hour 10mins

It's the pomegranate seeds gleaming like rubies on the surface of this fragrant rice pilaf that makes it seem bejewelled, but if you find these hard to get, the dish is still fabulous without them. After all, some things may polish up real nice but it's what underneath that counts.

★ FUN FACT ★

The music video for 'Bejeweled' was written and directed by Taylor Swift. This play on the Cinderella fairytale features an appearance from burlesque artist, Dita von Teese, with longtime writing partner and producer, Jack Antonoff playing the role of 'Prince Jack'!

BEJEWELED RICE PILAF

★ INGREDIENTS ★

2 teaspoons cumin seeds

2 teaspoons coriander seeds

10 cardamom pods

3 tablespoons olive oil

500g (1lb) shoulder of lamb, diced

2 red onions, sliced

25g (1oz) fresh root ginger, grated

2 garlic cloves, crushed

½ teaspoon ground turmeric

200g (7oz) red or brown rice

600ml (1 pint) lamb stock or chicken stock

40g (1½ oz) pine nuts

75g (3oz) ready-to-eat dried apricots, thinly sliced

50g (2oz) rocket

2 tablespoons pomegranate seeds

salt and pepper

★ METHOD ★

1. Grind the cumin seeds, coriander seeds and cardamom pods using a pestle and mortar until the cardamom pods have opened to release the seeds. Discard the shells.
2. Heat the oil in a small, sturdy roasting pan and fry the spices for 30 seconds. Add the lamb and onions and toss with the spices. Transfer to a preheated oven, 180°C (350°F), Gas Mark 4, and cook for 40 minutes until the lamb and onions are browned.
3. Return the pan to the hob and stir in the ginger, garlic, turmeric and rice. Add the stock and bring to the boil. Cover with a lid or foil and cook over the lowest setting for about 30 minutes until the rice is tender and the stock has been absorbed.
4. Stir in the pine nuts and apricots and season to taste. Scatter with the rocket and fold in very lightly. Scatter over the pomegranate seeds. Serve immediately.

SWEET NOTHING POTATO SOUP

SERVES 4 | PREP: 20mins | COOKING TIME: 20-25mins

This is a comforting dish to savour with someone who really deserves your love and attention. Take yourself into the kitchen and hum along as the simple ingredients transform into a sweet and silky soup.

SWEET NOTHING POTATO SOUP

★ INGREDIENTS ★

2 tablespoons vegetable oil

1 red onion, chopped

1 red pepper, deseeded and chopped

550g (1lb 2oz) sweet potatoes, peeled and chopped

¼ teaspoon ground cumin

8 baby tomatoes

1.2 litres (2 pints) vegetable stock

25g (1oz) creamed coconut

salt and pepper

natural yogurt, to serve

coriander sprigs, to garnish

★ METHOD ★

1. Heat the oil in a saucepan over a medium heat, add the onion and pepper and cook for 3–4 minutes. Stir in the sweet potatoes, cumin and tomatoes, and cook for a further 3–4 minutes.
2. Pour in the stock, bring to the boil and simmer for 12 minutes. Stir in the creamed coconut and cook for a further 4–5 minutes. Using a hand-held blender, blend the soup until smooth.
3. Season with salt and pepper and serve topped with a dollop of natural yogurt and a coriander sprig.

★ FUN FACT ★

'Sweet Nothing' was co-written with William Bowery, a pseudonym for the actor Joe Alwyn. While Alwyn and Taylor were in a relationship, he co-wrote and produced tracks on *Folklore*, which went on to win a Grammy Award for Album of the Year in 2021.

CORN-ELIA STREET FRITTERS

SERVES 16 | PREP: 20mins | COOKING TIME: 5mins

If you had a spare $18 million in 2023, you could have bought the Cornelia Street apartment that Taylor rented between 2016–2017! Located in the West Village area of Manhattan in New York City, the three-storey property has a basement gym and pool, four bedrooms, five bathrooms and a spacious roof terrace. The luxurious kitchen would be the perfect place to cook these sweetcorn fritters, so why not grab a piece of the superstar lifestyle with this laid-back lunch?

CORN-ELIA STREET FRITTERS

★ INGREDIENTS ★

FOR THE FRITTERS

125g (4oz) plain flour

1 egg

150ml (¼ pint) milk

400g (13oz) canned sweetcorn, drained

salt and pepper

4 tablespoons sunflower oil

ready-made guacamole, to serve

lime wedges, to serve

FOR THE SALSA

3 ripe tomatoes, chopped

2 spring onions, chopped

pinch of caster sugar

2 tablespoons ready-made French dressing

★ METHOD ★

1. Place the flour in a bowl, make a well in the centre and break in the egg. Gradually add the milk, mixing with a hand whisk to make a smooth, thick batter. Stir in the sweetcorn and season with salt and pepper.
2. Heat the oil in a large frying pan, add generous spoonfuls of the batter and fry, in batches, for about 5 minutes, turning once, until golden and crisp. Drain on kitchen paper.
3. To make the salsa, place the tomatoes in a bowl and crush lightly with a fork. Add the spring onions, sugar and French dressing, season with salt and pepper and mix well. Serve with the sweetcorn fritters, guacamole, and wedge of lime.

YOU BELONG WITH BRIE

ANTIPASTI HERO

SERVES 4 | PREP 10mins

Thanks to TikTok, charcuterie boards have become a culinary trend that delivers every time, and we are HERE for it! Simply arrange your favourite antipasti ingredients on a large wooden board or slate (or your favourite plates) and serve as a sharing lunch. This is an easily scalable dish. Vary quantities according to the number of people eating.

ANTIPASTI HERO

★ INGREDIENTS ★

100g (3½ oz) marinated olives

75g (3oz) chargrilled marinated artichokes

50g (oz) chargrilled peppers

50g (2oz) sun-dried tomatoes

50g (2oz) marinated anchovies

100g (3½ oz) prosciutto

100g (3½ oz) salami

220g (7½ oz) mozzarella cheese

6 tablespoons extra-virgin olive oil

4 tablespoons aged balsamic vinegar

grissini breadsticks, to serve

★ METHOD ★

1. Arrange the antipasti ingredients on a large platter or board. When ready to eat, pour the olive oil and balsamic vinegar into separate bowls for dipping.
2. Serve with grissini breadsticks.

★ FUN FACT ★

Pop-culture fans alert! The song 'Anti-Hero' featured in the last episode of season 4 of Netflix's serial killer drama, *You*. The main character, Joe Goldberg, is played by Penn Badgeley, who co-starred with – and dated – Taylor's BFF, Blake Lively, in *Gossip Girl*!

PAPER ONION RINGS

SERVES 4 | PREP: 10mins | COOKING TIME: 1–2mins

We like shiny things, but we'd also marry a dish of onion rings when they always taste as good as this! Hot from the frier, these are absolutely the one you want.

PAPER ONION RINGS

★ INGREDIENTS ★

FOR THE ONION RINGS

4 large onions

vegetable oil, for deep-frying

FOR THE BEER BATTER

1 egg, separated

1 tablespoon olive oil

100ml (3½ fl oz) light beer such as lager, chilled

65g (2½ oz) plain flour

salt and pepper

★ METHOD ★

1. Slice the onions into 5mm (¼ inch) thick rings and separate out into rings. Keep the larger rings and save the smaller ones in the refrigerator for another recipe.
2. Make the batter next. Whisk together the egg yolk, oil, beer and flour in a bowl. Season with salt and pepper. In another clean, dry bowl, whisk the egg white until stiff, then gently fold into the batter until smooth and combined.
3. Heat 5cm (2 inch) of vegetable oil in a deep heavy-based saucepan or a deep-fat fryer to 180°–190°C (350°–375°F), or until a cube of bread dropped into the oil browns in 30 seconds.
4. Dip the onion rings, a few at a time, into the batter, then gently drop into the oil and deep-fry in batches for 1–2 minutes until golden. Remove very carefully using a slotted spoon and drain on kitchen paper. Serve at once while the onions are crisp and piping hot.

★ TOP TIP ★

If you're ever in Kentish Town, London, drop into Kentish Delight. This kebab shop became a hot location for Swifties after appearing in the video for 'End Game' and is filled with Taylor memorabilia!

BETTER THAN REVENGE SPICY JALAPEÑOS

SERVES 4 | PREP: 5mins | COOKING TIME: 12–15mins

Be prepared to make multiple batches of these oozy, cheesy peppers as they won't last long! Don't underestimate the heat coming from them but if you're in the mood for a little strategic revenge, keep in mind that some people don't deserve a warning about their spiciness. Just sayin' ...

★ FUN FACT ★

In 'Better Than Revenge' on *Speak Now (Taylor's Version)* in 2023, one line of the lyrics had been rewritten to reflect Taylor's adult perspective on losing a boyfriend to another girl.

BETTER THAN REVENGE SPICY JALAPEÑOS

★ INGREDIENTS ★

FOR THE JALAPEÑOS

12 jalapeño peppers, halved and seeded, stems intact

200g (7oz) cream cheese

1 teaspoon paprika

1 tablespoon chives, finely chopped

50g Cheddar cheese, grated

5 tablespoons Panko breadcrumbs

2 teaspoons garlic powder

FOR THE CHIPOTLE SAUCE

1 onion

3 tomatoes

2 garlic cloves, peeled and left whole

1 teaspoon chipotle paste

4 tablespoons Greek yogurt

2 tablespoons mayonnaise

salt and pepper

★ METHOD ★

1. Lay the jalapeños on a baking sheet in rows, cut side up.
2. Mix the cream cheese, paprika, chives and Cheddar together in a bowl. Fill each jalapeño with the cream cheese mixture.
3. Stir the breadcrumbs and garlic together and sprinkle over the top of the cheese mixture. Bake in a preheated oven, 200°C (400°F), Gas Mark 6, for 12–15 minutes until the topping is golden.
4. Make the chipotle sauce. Cook the onions in a large, dry nonstick frying pan, add the onion and cook for 5 minutes. Add the tomatoes and cook for a further 5 minutes, then add the garlic and continue to cook for 3 minutes, or until the ingredients are softened and charred.
5. Transfer to a food processor or blender and whizz to a smooth paste. Leave to cool, then add the chipotle paste, yogurt and mayonnaise and season to taste. Serve with the spicy jalapeños.

BUT DADDY I LOVE HUMMUS

SERVES 4 | PREP: 5mins

Hummus is a Middle Eastern dip which makes a versatile vegan option when served with vegetables or flatbread for lunch. It also works well as an accompaniment to spiced dishes such as the Bejeweled Lamb Pilaf (page 42). You should see their faces when you tell people this is homemade!

BUT DADDY I LOVE HUMMUS

★ INGREDIENTS ★

400 g (13oz) can chickpeas, drained and rinsed

1 tablespoon tahini paste

1 garlic clove, peeled

4 tablespoons Greek yogurt

1 tablespoon rose harissa paste, plus extra to drizzle

2 tablespoons lemon juice

salt and pepper

flatbread, to serve

crudités, to serve

★ METHOD ★

1. Place all the ingredients in a food processor, reserving a few chickpeas to garnish, and blend to a smooth paste. If the consistency is too thick, add a little warm water.
2. Season to taste, transfer to a serving bowl and garnish with the reserved chickpeas and a drizzle of extra harissa. Serve with warmed flatbread and fresh crudités.

★ FUN FACT ★

'But Daddy I Love Him', from 2024's *The Tortured Poets Department*, is considered by many to be a continuation of the romantic themes that Taylor covered in 'Love Story' (2008). Both songs describe a forbidden love and explore pushing back against parental and societal expectations. Thankfully, it all ends happily ever after both times!

DINNER

'MARRY ME' JULIET FETTUCCINI

SERVES 2 | PREP: 10mins | COOKING TIME: 12mins

Yes, this recipe really is so good you'll never have to eat alone! Keep your love story going by cooking this version of the viral 'marry me' pasta recipe and your partner will be down on one knee before you know it! While this recipe serves two, it's scalable enough to feed a stadium-sized number of friends and family. Welcome to your crowd-pleaser era!

★ FUN FACT ★

'Love Story' (2008) has been included in the set list on all of Taylor's tours and was inspired by a boy she introduced to her friends and family who nobody liked!

'MARRY ME' JULIET FETTUCCINI

★ INGREDIENTS ★

200g (7oz) fettuccini

1 tablespoon olive oil

1 onion, finely diced

2 garlic cloves, crushed

2 tablespoons tomato purée

75g (3oz) sun-dried tomatoes (in oil), finely chopped

½ teaspoon dried oregano

½ teaspoon dried thyme

1 teaspoon paprika

½ teaspoon chilli flakes (optional)

zest and juice of ½ lemon

75g (3oz) baby spinach leaves

175g (6oz) mascarpone cheese

1 cup of reserved pasta water

50g (2oz) freshly grated Parmesan

½ bunch fresh basil leaves

salt and pepper

★ METHOD ★

1. Boil a large pan of water and cook the fettuccini according to the packet instructions until it reaches the al dente stage.
2. At the same time, heat the olive oil in a large frying pan and fry the onion and garlic for 1–2 minutes. Add the tomato purée, sun-dried tomatoes, oregano, thyme, paprika, chilli flakes (if using), lemon zest and juice, and salt and pepper. Stir for 2–3 minutes.
3. Add the spinach to the pan and continue to stir for 1–2 minutes as the leaves wilt, making sure the sauce doesn't catch on the bottom of the pan. Stir in the mascarpone and allow it to melt down.
4. Carefully add the drained fettuccini to the pan and stir everything together. Add a small splash of reserved pasta water at a time until the sauce reaches a velvety consistency that coats the pasta.
5. Stir in half of the parmesan, then serve. Top each bowl with the remaining parmesan and a few of the basil leaves.

SNAKE AND ALE PIE

SERVES 4 | PREP: 40mins, plus cooling

COOKING TIME: 1hour 40mins

Steak and ale pie is a classic British dish, and in honour of all the ways in which Taylor has used her haters' choice of snake emoji to her own advantage, this recipe has been renamed – because we love to see it!

★ FUN FACT ★

Taylor had the last laugh by using snake imagery in her costumes and sets from the Reputation era, especially during performances of 'Look What You Made Me Do'. Reclaim your narrative, Queen!

SNAKE AND ALE PIE

★ INGREDIENTS ★

2 tablespoons vegetable oil

450g (14½ oz) lean braising steak, cut into small pieces

225g (7½ oz) ox kidney, cored, trimmed and cut into small chunks

1 onion, thinly sliced

100g (3½ oz) chestnut mushrooms, quartered

2 tablespoons plain flour, plus extra for dusting

450ml (¾ pint) hot beef stock

150ml (¼ pint) ale

400g (13oz) ready-made shortcrust pastry

beaten egg, for glazing

salt and pepper

★ METHOD ★

1. Heat 1 tablespoon of the oil in a large frying pan on the hob and fry the beef, in batches, until browned on all sides, draining each batch to a plate. Add the kidney to the pan, fry for a further 5 minutes then drain. Add the remaining oil, onion and mushrooms to the pan and fry gently for a further 5 minutes.
2. Return all the ingredients to the pan, including any juices from the beef, and sprinkle in the flour, stirring for 1 minute. Add the stock and ale. Bring to the boil. Season and transfer to a casserole dish.
3. Cover the dish with a lid or foil and place in a preheated oven, 160°C (325°F), Gas Mark 3. Cook for about 2 hours or until the meat feels tender. Check the seasoning and leave to cool before transferring the mixture to one large pie dish.
4. Roll the pastry out on a lightly floured surface and cut out a lid about 1cm (½ inch) larger than the dish. Position the pastry over the filling, crimping it around the edges to seal. Brush the pastry with beaten egg to glaze, then return to the oven.
5. Increase the temperature to 225°C (437°F) and cook for 35 minutes.

PENNSYLVANIA PHILLY CHEESESTEAK

SERVES 2 | PREP: 10mins, plus freezing

COOKING TIME: 10mins

Partially freezing the steak helps it to cut into the wafer-thin slices that give the Philly Cheesesteak its unique texture and character. Using words that cut like a knife is one of Taylor's unique characteristics, so it's fitting that she is 'almost' a Philadelphia native, having been born just over an hour away in Reading, Pennsylvania. She was also a lifelong support of the Philadelphia Eagles American Football team until beginning her relationship with Kansas City Chiefs player, Travis Kelce, in 2023.

PENNSYLVANIA PHILLY CHEESESTEAK

★ INGREDIENTS ★

500g (1lb) boneless rib eye or skirt steak

1 tablespoon oil

1 onion, diced

125g provolone cheese, thinly sliced

salt and pepper

2 white sub or hot dog rolls

★ METHOD ★

1. Cut the steak in half and freeze the pieces on a tray for just under an hour.
2. Remove the steak from the freezer. Shave into 2½ mm (⅛ inch) slices, or as close to this as you can, using a very sharp knife.
3. Heat the oil in a heavy-based frying pan or skillet until it is almost smoking. Add the steak and onions and cook without stirring for 4–5 minutes. Stir and separate the steak slices and move briskly around the pan for a further 2–3 minutes until cooked and mostly brown all over.
4. Reserve four slices of the cheese and stir the rest into the pan, along with the seasoning. Allow the cheese to melt slightly.
5. Divide the mixture into two long piles, roughly the length of the rolls. Top with the reserved cheese and allow to soften slightly, then scoop the cooked mixture into sub rolls which have been sliced in half lengthways. Serve immediately.

MILDEST DREAMS VEGETABLE KORMA

SERVES 4-6 | PREP: 15mins | COOKING TIME: 40mins

Ah-ah, ha! Even if you aren't a fan of spicy food this mild vegetable curry should change your mind. It's a vegan recipe which can be adapted for vegetarians by adding cubes of paneer cheese along with the peas towards the end of the recipe. (Fry these lightly first, to create a crust which helps the paneer hold its shape.)

★ FUN FACT ★

As well as 'Wildest Dreams', *1989* (2014) spawned six other hit singles including 'Bad Blood' featuring Kendrick Lamar. Lamar performed at the 2025 Super Bowl halftime show, watched by Taylor who was supporting her Chiefs player boyfriend, Travis Kelce!

MILDEST DREAMS VEGETABLE KORMA

★ INGREDIENTS ★

2 tablespoons sunflower oil
8 shallots, finely chopped
1 teaspoon ground cumin
1 teaspoon ground coriander
1 teaspoon ground turmeric
1 teaspoon chilli powder
1 teaspoon garam masala
4 ripe plum tomatoes, roughly chopped
1 red pepper, cut into large chunks
1 green pepper, cut into large chunks
2 baking potatoes, peeled and cubed
1 small cauliflower, cut into florets
2 teaspoons crushed garlic
2 red chillies, deseeded and finely sliced
2 tablespoons tomato purée
150ml (¼ pint) water
200ml (7fl oz) coconut milk
200g (7oz) frozen peas
finely chopped fresh coriander, to garnish
poppadums, to serve

★ METHOD ★

1. Heat the oil in a large nonstick wok or frying pan, add the shallots and stir-fry for 2–3 minutes. Add the ground spices and stir-fry for 1 minute.
2. Add the tomatoes, peppers, potato, cauliflower, garlic, chillies, tomato purée and measured water and bring to the boil. Reduce the heat and simmer, covered, for 25–30 minutes, or until the potatoes are tender to the tip of a knife.
3. Stir in the coconut milk and peas and gently simmer, uncovered, for 5 minutes or until the peas are cooked.
4. Season well, remove from the heat and stir in the coriander just before serving. Serve immediately with poppadums.

COWBOY LIKE BEANS

SERVES 4-6 | PREP: 15mins, plus overnight soaking

COOKING TIME: 2 hours

Everyone will think you have some special tricks up your sleeve when you hit them with this classic American recipe. Play *Evermore* as your dinner time soundtrack to lasso your own cowboy!

For Boston Beans (Vegetarian Version), replace the haricot beans with the same quantity of butter beans. Replace the bacon and pork with 12 vegetarian sausages and set aside at the end of Step 3. Add the veggie sausages back to the pan at the start of Step 5.

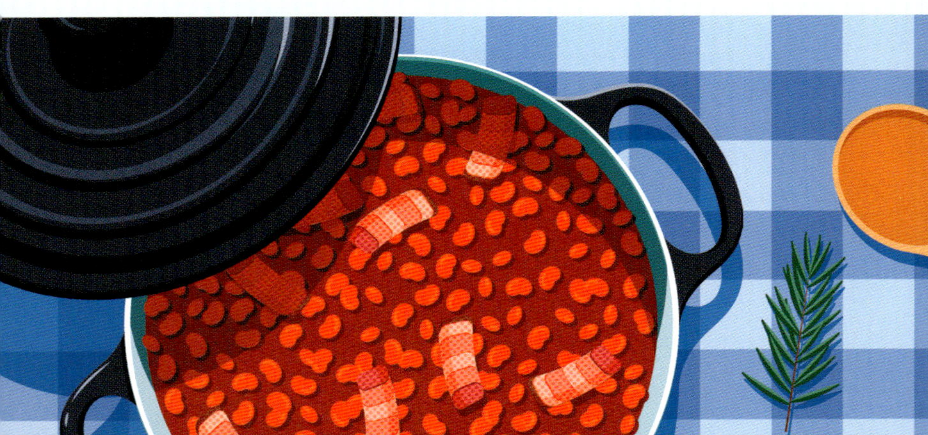

COWBOY LIKE BEANS

★ INGREDIENTS ★

300g (10oz) haricot beans

15g (½ oz) butter

200g (7oz) smoked bacon lardons

375g (12oz) lean diced pork

1 onion, chopped

1 tablespoon chopped thyme or rosemary

400g (13oz) can chopped tomatoes

3 tablespoons black treacle

2 tablespoons tomato purée

2 tablespoons grainy mustard

1 tablespoon Worcestershire sauce

salt and pepper

★ METHOD ★

1. Put the beans in a bowl, cover with cold water and leave to soak overnight.
2. Drain the beans and put in a flameproof casserole. Cover with water and bring to the boil. Reduce the heat and simmer gently for 15–20 minutes or until the beans have softened slightly. Test by removing a few on a fork and squeezing them gently – they should give a little. Drain the beans.
3. Wipe out the dish and melt the butter. Add the bacon and pork and fry gently for 10 minutes until beginning to brown. Add the onion and cook for a further 5 minutes.
4. Stir in the drained beans, thyme or rosemary and tomatoes. Add enough water to just cover the ingredients and bring to the boil. Cover with a lid and transfer to a preheated oven, 150°C (300°F), Gas Mark 2. Cook for about 1 hour or until the beans are very tender.
5. Mix together the treacle, tomato purée, mustard, Worcestershire sauce and seasoning. Stir into the beans and return to the oven for a further 30 minutes.

THE TORTELLINI POETS DEPARTMENT

SERVES 4 | PREP: 10mins | COOKING TIME: 8–12mins

You don't need to decode anything with this dish, it's simply as straightforward as can be. The only challenging ingredient is the nutmeg – if you don't have it, the flavour of the sauce will be less complex but adding extra parmesan will help to overcome this.

★ INGREDIENTS ★

15g (½ oz) unsalted butter

150g (5oz) shelled peas, defrosted if frozen

75g (3oz) ham, cut into strips

300g (10oz) crème fraîche

large pinch of freshly grated nutmeg, optional

500g (1lb) fresh spinach and ricotta or meat tortellini

40g (1½ oz) Parmesan cheese, freshly grated, plus extra to serve

★ METHOD ★

1. Melt the butter in a large frying pan over a medium heat until it begins to sizzle. Add the peas and ham and cook, stirring, for 3–4 minutes if using fresh peas, or just 1 minute if using defrosted frozen peas.
2. Stir in the crème fraîche, add the nutmeg if using, and season with salt and pepper. Bring to the boil and boil for 2 minutes until slightly thickened.
3. Cook the tortellini in a large saucepan of salted boiling water according to the packet instructions until it is al dente. Drain and toss into the creamy sauce with the Parmesan. Gently stir to combine and serve at once with a scattering of Parmesan.

★ FUN FACT ★

The Tortured Poets Department is the first album in Spotify history to have more than 300 million streams in a single day. (19th April, 2024, stat lovers.) 'Fortnight' featuring Post Malone also became Spotify's most-streamed song in a single day on the same date!

FEARLESS FISH TACOS

SERVES 4 | PREP: 20mins | COOKING TIME: 10–15mins

Tacos don't get better than this. Crispy spiced fish and tangy homemade tartare sauce wrapped in a soft taco shell: flawless! Take extra care when frying the fish in the hot oil and if time is tight, using store-bought tartare sauce isn't the end of the world.

★ FUN FACT ★

Fearless was the best-selling country album of 2009 and won Taylor four Grammy Awards, including Best Country Album and Album of the Year. When re-released as *Fearless (Taylor's Version)* in 2021 – the number of tracks increased from 13 to 27!

FEARLESS FISH TACOS

★ INGREDIENTS ★

FOR THE FISH AND BATTER

100g (3½ oz) plain flour

2 teaspoons ground cumin

1 teaspoon chilli powder

2 teaspoons dried oregano

200ml (7fl oz) cold water

400g (13oz) white fish, skinned and sliced into thick strips

vegetable oil, for deep-frying

salt and pepper

FOR THE TARTARE SAUCE

100g (3½ oz) mayonnaise

1 fresh jalapeño chilli, chopped

1 teaspoon capers, drained

1 small gherkin, finely chopped

grated zest and juice of ½ lime

handful of coriander leaves, chopped

TO SERVE

¼ red cabbage, finely sliced

8 corn tortillas

lime wedges

★ METHOD ★

1. Place the flour, spices, oregano and measured water in a shallow dish and stir together until it resembles thick cream. Season the fish, then dip in the flour mixture until well coated.
2. Fill a large saucepan one-third full of oil and heat to 180–190°C (350–375°F), or until a cube of bread browns in 15 seconds. Let any excess batter drip away from the fish, then deep-fry in batches for 3–5 minutes until golden and crisp.
3. Make the tartare sauce by mixing all the ingredients in a bowl.
4. Toss the cabbage with a little salt and a dash of lime juice. Divide among the tortillas, add the fish and tartare sauce. Serve with lime wedges.

LOVER-MICELLI SOUP

SERVES 4-6 | PREP: 15mins | COOKING TIME: 55mins

There's nothing like a bowl of soup as a comforting dinner option during the cold winter months. Adapt to suit the veggies you have available or leave out the chicken to make this recipe suitable for vegetarians or vegans. Wrapping up in a cosy cardigan while this is puttering away on the stove would also be very acceptable, especially if you've been lucky enough to get your hands on one of the sold out 'Lover' cardigans released by Taylor in January 2025.

LOVER-MICELLI SOUP

★ INGREDIENTS ★

2 tablespoons olive oil

1 onion, thinly sliced

2 carrots, diced

2 celery sticks, diced

2 garlic cloves, peeled

1 potato, peeled and diced

125g (4oz) frozen peas

1 courgette, diced

125 (4oz) French beans, trimmed and cut into 3.5 cm (1½ inch) pieces

125 g (4oz) tomatoes, skinned and chopped

1.2 litres (2 pints) vegetable stock

300g (10oz) shredded cooked chicken

75g (3oz) thin noodles or vermicelli

salt and black pepper

★ METHOD ★

1. Heat the olive oil in a large, heavy-based saucepan over a low heat, add the onion, carrots, celery and garlic and cook, stirring occasionally, for 10 minutes. Add the potato, peas or broad beans, courgette and French beans and cook, stirring frequently, for 2 minutes. Add the tomatoes and chicken, season with salt and pepper and cook for a further 2 minutes.
2. Pour in the stock and bring to the boil. Reduce the heat and gently simmer for 15–20 minutes, or until all the vegetables are very tender and the chicken is heated through.
3. Add the noodles to the soup and cook, stirring frequently, until they are soft. Adjust the seasoning before serving.

BILLBOARD CHEESEBOARD
WITH GREEN TOMATO CHUTNEY

MAKES 4 JARS | PREP: 15mins

COOKING TIME: 1¼–1½hours

When cutting the cheese, aim for uniform-sized pieces and intersperse the items you're serving with them, such as grapes or crackers, for the most aesthetic effect. Choose your own selection of cheeses to customise your board and serve with grapes and crackers.

BILLBOARD CHEESEBOARD

★ INGREDIENTS ★

FOR THE CHEESEBOARD

250–400g (8–13oz) of 5 or 6 of your favourite cheeses, cut into slices or cubes, with a mixture of:

Hard cheese, such as Cheddar

Blue cheese, such as Stilton

Crumbly cheese, such as Caerphilly

Soft cheese, such as brie or Camembert

An artisan cheese, such as one which is smoked or spiced

FOR THE GREEN TOMATO CHUTNEY

1kg (2lb) green tomatoes, chopped

500g (1lb) onions, finely chopped

500g (1lb) cooking apples, peeled, cored and chopped

2 fresh green chillies, finely chopped

2 garlic cloves, crushed

1 teaspoon ground ginger

generous pinch of ground cloves

generous pinch of ground turmeric

50g (2oz) raisins

250g (8oz) soft dark brown sugar

300ml (½ pint) white wine vinegar

★ METHOD ★

1. Combine the tomatoes, onions, apples and chillies to a large pan. Add the garlic, ginger, cloves and turmeric, then stir in the raisins, sugar and vinegar.
2. Bring to the boil, then reduce the heat and simmer, covered, for 1¼–1½ hours, or until the chutney has thickened, stirring frequently.
3. Ladle into dry, sterilized jars. Disperse any air pockets with a skewer or small knife and cover with screw-top lids. Label and leave to mature in a cool, dark place for at least 3 weeks.

★ FUN FACT ★

Taylor has 49 Billboard Music Awards, making her the most-awarded artist at the time of writing!

(198)9 BEAN AND HERB SALAD

SERVES 4 | PREP: 15mins | COOKING TIME: 12–15mins

Get ready for your squad to enjoy (198)9 key ingredients in this vegan-friendly bean and herb salad, which makes a filling dinner or flavoursome side dish. Each one adds something different to the mix, much like the special guests who appeared on-stage during the 1989 Tour. From actors and models such as Hailee Steinfeld, Julia Roberts and Gigi Hadid, to performers including Lorde, Selena Gomez and John Legend, this was absolutely Taylor's #SquadGoals era!

(198)9 BEAN AND HERB SALAD

★ INGREDIENTS ★

300g (10oz) small new potatoes, scrubbed and halved

200g (7oz) fine green beans, topped and tailed and halved

400g (13oz) can cannellini beans, drained and rinsed

200g (7oz) can butter beans, drained and rinsed

75g (3oz) pitted black olives, sliced

½ small red onion, thinly sliced

4 tablespoons extra virgin olive oil

grated rind and juice of 1 large lemon

pinch of caster sugar

2 tablespoons chopped mint

2 tablespoons chopped flat leaf parsley

2 tablespoons chopped dill

salt and black pepper

★ METHOD ★

1. Cook the potatoes in a large saucepan of boiling water for 12–15 minutes until tender, adding the green beans for the last 3 minutes. Drain and refresh under cold running water.
2. Place the cannellini beans, butter beans, olives and onion in a large bowl and stir in the potatoes and green beans.
3. Whisk together the oil, lemon rind and juice, sugar and salt and pepper in a jug, then stir in the chopped herbs. Pour over the bean and potato mixture and toss well before serving.

I CAN DO IT WITH A BROKEN TART

SERVES 6 | PREP: 45mins, plus chilling and cooling

COOKING TIME: 50–55mins

Never fear, using ready-made pastry will still have the crowd chanting "More!" once they taste this amazing tart. 'I Can Do It With a Broken Heart' was the second single from *The Tortured Poets Department*, which was written while Taylor was performing on the Eras Tour in 2023. Its lyrics relate to how Taylor still had to perform while dealing with the emotional fallout of her break-up with boyfriend of six years, Joe Alwyn.

★ INGREDIENTS ★

1 pack ready-made shortcrust pastry

50g (2oz) butter

6 shallots, finely chopped

2 garlic cloves, crushed

2 teaspoons chopped thyme

350g (11½ oz) mixed mushrooms, trimmed and sliced

300ml (½ pint) soured cream

3 eggs, lightly beaten

25g (1oz) Parmesan cheese, freshly grated

salt and pepper

salad leaves, to serve

★ METHOD ★

1. Roll the pastry out on a lightly floured work surface. Use to line a 25cm (10 inch) fluted flan tin. Prick the base with a fork and chill for 30 minutes. Line the pastry with nonstick baking paper and pour in sufficient ceramic baking beans or uncooked rice to cover the base. Bake in a preheated oven, 200°C (400°F), Gas Mark 6, for 15 minutes. Remove the paper and beans/rice and bake for a further 15 minutes. Leave to cool.
2. Meanwhile, melt the butter in a frying pan, add the shallots, garlic and thyme and cook over a low heat, stirring frequently, for 5 minutes. Increase the heat, add the mushrooms and salt and pepper and cook, stirring, for 4–5 minutes until browned. Leave to cool. Scatter over the tart case.
3. Beat the soured cream, eggs, Parmesan and salt and pepper in a jug and pour over the top. Bake for 20–25 minutes until golden and just set. Serve warm with salad leaves.

ALL TOO WELLINGTON

SERVES 6 | PREP: 30mins | COOKING TIME: 55mins

Beef Wellington is a classic English dinner dish believed to be named after the first Duke of Wellington who defeated Napoleon at the Battle of Waterloo. You won't be asking too much if you go in for another rare slice (and you'll remember it all too well afterwards).

★ FUN FACT ★

'All Too Well' was originally ad-libbed by Taylor and her musicians during a rehearsal session when she was 21 and getting over her break-up with actor, Jake Gyllenhaal.

★ INGREDIENTS ★

1.5kg (3lb) beef fillet (preferably cut from the middle of the fillet)

50g (2oz) butter

2 small onions, finely chopped

300g (10oz) chestnut mushrooms, chopped

2 tablespoons brandy

500g (1lb) ready-made puff pastry

a little flour, for dusting

200g (7oz) smooth chicken pâté

beaten egg, to glaze

salt and pepper

★ METHOD ★

1. Trim off the excess fat and season the beef with salt and pepper. Melt the butter in a frying pan and once it is bubbling, quickly sear the beef so that it is brown on all sides. Transfer it to a roasting tin, reserving the fat in the pan, and roast in a preheated oven, 200°C (400°F), Gas Mark 6, for 20 minutes. Leave to cool.
2. Fry the onions in the pan for 5 minutes while the beef is cooking. Add the mushrooms and a little seasoning and fry until the moisture has evaporated. Add the brandy and fry for a further minute.
3. Thinly roll out the pastry to a large rectangle on a lightly floured surface. Spread the top of the meat with the chicken pâté, then press a thick layer of the mushroom mixture over the top. Turn the beef on to the pastry and spread with the remaining mushrooms.
4. Brush the pastry with beaten egg and bring it up over the fillet to enclose the meat completely, trimming off any bulky areas at the corners. Place it onto a lightly greased baking sheet, join side down. Brush with more of the egg. Bake for 35 minutes, then stand for 20 minutes before carving.

YOU BELONG WITH BRIE

STEW ROMANTICS

SERVES 4 | PREP: 15mins | COOKING TIME: 55mins

Most of the rumours are true – this is a veggie take on a traditional French Provençal stew. You'll be knocked off your feet by the soft liquorice taste of the fennel which complements the sweetness of the peppers and saltiness of the olives. Making it the day before will allow the rich flavours to develop even more overnight.

★ INGREDIENTS ★

4 tablespoons extra virgin olive oil, plus extra for drizzling

1 large red onion, sliced

4 garlic cloves, chopped

2 teaspoons ground coriander

1 tablespoon chopped thyme

1 fennel bulb, trimmed and sliced

1 red pepper, cored, deseeded and sliced

500g (1lb) vine-ripened tomatoes, diced

300ml (½ pint) vegetable stock

125g (4oz) Niçoise olives

2 tablespoons chopped parsley

slices of crusty bread

salt and black pepper

★ METHOD ★

1. Heat the oil in a large saucepan and add the onion, garlic, coriander and thyme. Cook over a medium heat, stirring frequently, for 5 minutes until the onion is softened. Add the fennel and red pepper and cook, stirring frequently, for 10 minutes until softened.
2. Stir in the tomatoes, stock and salt and pepper. Bring to the boil, then reduce the heat. Cover and simmer gently for 30 minutes. Stir in the olives and parsley and simmer, uncovered, for a further 10 minutes.
3. Meanwhile, heat a ridged griddle pan until hot. Add the bread slices and cook until toasted and charred on both sides. Drizzle liberally with oil. Serve with the stew.

★ FUN FACT ★

'New Romantic' was the name given to synth-pop music from the 1970s and 1980s. *1989* is widely-described as a synth-pop album as it used more electronic arrangements and continued the evolution of Taylor's sound from country to pop.

BANGERS AND NASHVILLE

SERVES 6 | PREP: 30mins | COOKING TIME: 30mins

'Bangers' is a British slang term for sausages and comes from they way they used to sometimes explode while cooking! It's also a great word to describe so many of Taylor's songs! Bangers and mash is a quintessential British dinner, and is a fitting tribute to the years Taylor spent living in London.

★ FUN FACT ★

Taylor's whole family relocated from Pennsylvania to Nashville, Tennessee when she was 13 as Taylor was convinced this was where she needed to be to hone her songwriting skills. It's safe to say that move paid off!

BANGERS AND NASHVILLE

★ INGREDIENTS ★

FOR THE SAUSAGES

8 sausages

2 onions, cut into wedges

2 dessert apples, cored and cut into wedges

1 tablespoon olive oil

FOR THE MUSTARD MASH

1kg (2lb) potatoes, quartered

75g (3oz) butter

1–2 tablespoons wholegrain mustard

1 garlic clove, crushed

salt and pepper

1 large bunch of parsley, chopped

dash of olive oil

FOR THE GRAVY

1 tablespoon plain flour

200ml (7fl oz) chicken stock

★ METHOD ★

1. Boil the potatoes for 15–20 minutes until tender.
2. Meanwhile, grill the sausages at a medium heat for 8–10 minutes, turning frequently for an even colour. Add the onion and apple wedges to the pan and drizzle them with the olive oil. Transfer to a preheated oven, 190°C (375°F), Gas Mark 5, for 10 minutes or until the onion and apples have softened.
3. Drain and mash the potatoes. Add the butter, mustard, garlic and salt and pepper, then stir in the parsley and olive oil.
4. Pour off the excess fat from the pan to leave about 1 tablespoon of juices, then mix in the flour. Gradually stir in the stock, bring to the boil and stir until thickened. Season and strain the gravy into a jug, then pour over the sausages and mash.

DESSERT

BOMBALURINA BANOFFEE PIE

SERVES 6 | PREP: 35mins, plus chilling and cooling

COOKING TIME: 18mins

This smoothly sweet treat is named after the character played by Taylor Swift in the 2019 movie adaptation of the legendary musical, *Cats.* Bombalurina is sleek, confident and attention-grabbing, much like a banoffee pie!

★ FUN FACT ★

Taylor was inspired to take the role in *Cats* because of her love for her own fur-babies – Meredith Grey, Olivia Benson and Benjamin Button – who she describes as "… very dignified … independent … [and] capable of dealing with their own life." Who does that remind you of?

BOMBALURINA BANOFFEE PIE

★ INGREDIENTS ★

200g (7oz) unsalted butter

2 tablespoons golden syrup

250g (8oz) digestive biscuits, crushed

100g (3½ oz) dark muscovado sugar

400g (13oz) can full-fat condensed milk

300ml (½ pint) double cream

3 small bananas, thinly sliced

plain dark chocolate, grated, to decorate

★ METHOD ★

1. Melt half the butter and all of the syrup in a saucepan, add the biscuit crumbs and mix well. Tip into a greased 20cm (8 inch) springform tin and press evenly over the base and up the sides almost to the tin's top. Chill.
2. Heat the remaining butter and the sugar in a nonstick frying pan until the butter has melted and the sugar dissolved. Add the condensed milk and cook over a medium heat, stirring continuously, for 4–5 minutes until the mixture thickens and it begins to smell of caramel.
3. Take the pan off the heat and leave the mixture to cool for 1–2 minutes. Pour a thin layer of caramel over the biscuit base, then add a layer of sliced bananas. Continue layering until all the filling ingredients are used. Allow to cool completely, then chill for at least 2 hours.
4. Whip the cream until it forms soft peaks. Spoon over the toffee and banana layer. Loosen the edge of the biscuit crust with a palette knife, then remove the tin and transfer the pie to a serving plate. Sprinkle with grated chocolate and serve cut into wedges.

LOOK WHAT YOU MADE ME FONDUE

SERVES 8 | PREP: 20mins

A chocolate fondue is a classic sharing dessert, although once you've made it once (and checked it twice) you might find you want to keep this prize just for yourself. The choice of what you dip in it is up to you – marshmallows and strawberries never go out of style, but some other new contenders may wish to share centre stage, such as pretzels or sliced fruits. There's enough to go around so you'll all get yours. Now, I'mma let you finish your fondue in peace ...

★ INGREDIENTS ★

FOR THE FONDUE

400g (13oz) dark chocolate, broken into small pieces

25g (1oz) unsalted butter

150ml (¼ pint) double cream

50ml (2fl oz) milk

FOR DIPPING

fresh strawberries

marshmallows

apple slices

grapes

plain or lightly salted pretzel chips

★ METHOD ★

1. In a small saucepan gently heat the chocolate, butter, cream and milk, stirring occasionally, until the chocolate is melted and the sauce is glossy and smooth. Transfer to a warmed bowl or fondue pot.
2. Thread your dipping ingredients on to skewers, dip into the dark chocolate fondue and eat straight away.

ILLICIT ECLAIRS

MAKES 18 | PREP: 40mins, plus cooling

COOKING TIME: 15mins

You might have eaten a bakery éclair a million times, but there's no big secret to making them yourself. These instructions will remove the mystery and make everything clear – the only dangerous thing about them is how they'll leave you wanting more. *Rolling Stone* magazine described 'Illicit Affairs' as "the underrated romantic tragedy of *Folklore*." Stay strong, Swifties.

ILLICIT ECLAIRS

★ INGREDIENTS ★

FOR THE ÉCLAIRS

150ml (¼ pint) water

50g (2oz) butter

65g (2½ oz) plain flour, sifted

2 eggs, beaten

½ teaspoon vanilla essence

FOR THE FILLING

250ml (8 fl oz) double cream

2 tablespoons icing sugar

4 tablespoons whisky or coffee cream liqueur (such as Baileys)

FOR THE TOPPING

25 g (1oz) butter

100 g (3½ oz) dark chocolate

1 tablespoon icing sugar

2–3 teaspoons milk

★ METHOD ★

1. Heat the water and butter gently in a saucepan until melted. Bring to the boil then add the flour and beat until it forms a smooth ball that leaves the sides of the pan almost clean. Cool for 10 minutes.
2. Gradually mix the eggs and vanilla into the cooled pastry base until thick and smooth. Spoon the choux mixture into a large nylon piping bag fitted with a 1cm (½ inch) plain piping tube and pipe 7.5cm (3 inch) lines on to a lightly greased baking sheet.
3. Bake in a preheated oven, 200°C (400°F), Gas Mark 6, for 15 minutes until well risen. Make a slit in the side of each éclair for the steam to escape then return to the turned-off oven for 5 minutes. Leave to cool.
4. Whip the cream then gradually whisk in the icing sugar and liqueur. Slit each éclair lengthways and spoon or pipe in the cream.
5. Gently heat the butter, chocolate and icing sugar together in a small saucepan until just melted. Stir in the milk then spoon over the top of the éclairs. Serve the same day.

CRUEL SUMMER PUDDING

SERVES 8 | PREP: 15mins, plus chilling

COOKING TIME: 10–15mins

Summer Pudding is a classic English dessert and is deceptively simple to make for such a showstopping outcome. For what it's worth, take care when turning it out of its dish to ensure sure it keeps its shape – it's easily breakable but the risk is worth the reward. If using frozen fruits, thaw thoroughly before using.

★ FUN FACT ★

Although 'Cruel Summer' comes from 2019's *Lover*, it didn't reach the top of the charts until four years later when Taylor's record company, Republic Records, promoted the track as if it was a new single.

CRUEL SUMMER PUDDING

★ INGREDIENTS ★

250g (8oz) redcurrants, plus extra sprigs to decorate (optional)

125g (4oz) caster sugar

250g (8oz) strawberries

125g (4oz) raspberries

125g (4oz) blackberries

8 slices of white bread, crusts removed

★ METHOD ★

1. Put the redcurrants and sugar in a heavy-based saucepan and cook over a low heat, stirring occasionally, for 10–15 minutes until tender. Add the blackberries, strawberries and raspberries, remove from the heat and leave to cool. Strain the fruit, reserving the juice.
2. Cut 3 rounds of bread the same diameter as a 900ml (1½ pint) pudding basin. Shape the remaining bread to fit around the side of the basin. Soak all the bread in the reserved fruit juice.
3. Line the base of the basin with one of the rounds, then arrange the shaped bread around the side. Pour in half the fruit and place another round of bread on top. Cover with the remaining fruit, then top with the remaining bread round.
4. Cover with a plate small enough to fit inside the basin and put a 500g (1lb) weight on top. Chill in the refrigerator overnight.
5. Turn out on to a serving plate, pour over any remaining fruit juice and decorate with a few redcurrant sprigs arranged on top of the pudding in the centre, if wished. Serve with whipped or pouring cream.

WELCOME TO NEW YORK CHEESECAKES

SERVES 6 | PREP: 15mins | COOKING TIME: 20mins

These mini cheesecakes really have been waiting for you! Unlike traditional cheesecakes, a New York cheesecake filling has a denser texture and richer flavour thanks to its combination of cream cheese and soured cream. It's basically the older, more mature sister of the cheesecake family.

★ INGREDIENTS ★

7g (3oz) digestive biscuits, crushed
25g (1oz) unsalted butter, melted
200g (7oz) light cream cheese
50g (2oz) caster sugar
50g (2oz) soured cream
finely grated zest of ½ lemon
1 teaspoon vanilla extract
1 tablespoon cornflour
2 eggs
raspberries, to serve
icing sugar, for dusting

NEW YORK

★ METHOD ★

1. Line a 6-hole muffin tin with paper cases. Stir the crushed biscuits into the melted butter and press into the bases of the cases. Chill while you make the filling.
2. Place the cream cheese, sugar, soured cream, lemon zest, vanilla extract, cornflour and eggs in a bowl and beat together.
3. Spoon the mixture over the biscuit bases and place in a preheated oven, 160°C (325°F), Gas Mark 3, for 20 minutes. Leave to cool in the tin for 5 minutes.
4. Remove the cheesecakes from the cases and place on a serving plate. Serve warm, decorated with raspberries and a dusting of icing sugar.

★ FUN FACT ★

Taylor has one younger sibling, Austin, who works in the movie industry. He is described by his sister as one of her "best pals". Awww!

CHAI TEABREAD

SERVES 6 | PREP: 30mins, plus chilling

COOKING TIME: 10–15mins

One of the things that Swifties know all too well about Taylor is that she loves to bake! Her handwritten recipe for Chai Sugar Cookies almost broke the internet when it was published on her Tumblr and became a festive fan favourite when she baked them for her 'living room parties' ahead of the release of *1989*. Listeners attending the '1989 Secret Sessions' during the festive season got to hear tracks from the upcoming album and eat baked goods made by Taylor herself. This chai-based recipe has all the right ingredients to become a spicy hit in your living room, too!

CHAI TEABREAD

★ INGREDIENTS ★

5 chai tea bags
300ml (½ pint) boiling water
250g (8oz) self-raising flour
1 teaspoon baking powder
150g (5oz) light muscovado sugar
300g (10oz) mixed dried fruit
50g (2oz) Brazil nuts, chopped
50g (2oz) butter
1 egg, beaten

★ METHOD ★

1. Stir the tea bags into the boiling water in a jug and leave to stand for 10 minutes.
2. Mix the flour, baking powder, sugar, dried fruit and nuts together in a bowl. Remove the tea bags from the water, pressing them against the side of the jug to squeeze out all the liquid. Thinly slice the butter into the water and stir until melted. Leave to cool slightly. Add to the dry ingredients with the egg and mix well.
3. Spoon the mixture into a greased and lined 1kg (2lb) or 1.3litre (2¼ pint) loaf tin and spread the mixture into the corners. Bake in a preheated oven, 160°C (325°F), Gas Mark 3, for 1¼ hours or until risen, firm and a skewer inserted into the centre comes out clean.
4. Loosen the cake at the ends and transfer to a wire rack. Peel off the lining paper and leave to cool before transferring to a serving plate.

DOUGHNUT BLAME ME

MAKES 10 | PREP: 30mins, plus 1½–2½ hours proving

COOKING TIME: 8–10mins

These doughuts are so amazing you'll be making them for the rest of your life! Nobody will blame you if they drive you crazy (but if they don't, maybe you're not doing them right)!

★ FUN FACT ★

'Don't Blame Me' references the character Daisy from F Scott Fitzgerald's *The Great Gatsby.* Fans might also spot references to *Jane Eyre*, *The Iliad*, *Alice in Wonderland* and *The Hunger Games* in other tracks.

DOUGHNUT BLAME ME

★ INGREDIENTS ★

450g (14½ oz) strong white bread flour
50g (2oz) caster sugar
1¼ teaspoons fast-action dried yeast
½ teaspoon salt
1 large egg, beaten
225ml (7½ fl oz) milk, warmed
2 teaspoons vanilla extract
25g (1oz) unsalted butter, softened
Rapeseed oil to fry
100 g (3½ oz) caster sugar
1 teaspoon ground cinnamon

★ METHOD ★

1. Place the flour, sugar, yeast and salt into the bowl of an electric stand mixer fitted with a dough hook. Whisk the egg, milk and vanilla extract together in a jug. Pour into the flour and mix on a medium speed for 8–10 minutes. Gradually add small amounts of the butter and continue to mix until the dough forms a soft ball.
2. Transfer the dough to a lightly oiled bowl and cover it with cling film. Leave in a warm place for around 1–1½ hours until the dough has doubled in size.
3. Turn the dough on to a floured surface and cut into 10 equal pieces. Shape each into a ball and space them, well apart, on a greased baking sheet. Cover loosely with oiled clingfilm and leave to rise in a warm place for 30–40 minutes.
4. Put 8cm (3 inches) of cooking oil in a large saucepan and heat until a small piece of bread turns golden in about 30 seconds. Fry the doughnuts, 3–4 at a time, for about 3 minutes, turning once until golden all over. Drain each batch onto kitchen paper.
5. Mix the sugar and cinnamon on a plate. Roll the doughnuts in the cinnamon sugar while still warm. Eat straight away.

RED VELVET CAKE

SERVES 8–10 | PREP: 30mins | COOKING TIME: 25–30mins

RED (2012) was Taylor Swift's fourth studio album, and the last one to be promoted as country music. It catapulted Taylor into the pop/rock spectrum thanks to mega-hits, '22', 'I Knew You Were Trouble' and 'We Are Never Getting Back Together'. *RED (Taylor's Version)*, contains a massive 30 tracks and has a running time of 2 hours and 10 minutes – which is more than long enough to make and bake this RED velvet cake!

RED VELVET CAKE

★ INGREDIENTS ★

FOR THE CAKE

250g (8oz) plain flour
2 tablespoons cocoa powder
1 teaspoon bicarbonate of soda
2 teaspoons baking powder
275g (9oz) caster sugar
1 teaspoon salt
200ml (7 fl oz) buttermilk
150ml (¼ pint) vegetable oil
100ml (3½ fl oz) water
2 teaspoons white wine vinegar
2 teaspoons vanilla extract
2 eggs
1 tablespoon red food colouring

FOR THE FROSTING

150g (5oz) unsalted butter
300g (8oz) full-fat cream cheese
2 teaspoons vanilla extract
150g (12oz) icing sugar

★ METHOD ★

1. Grease and line two 20cm (8 inch) cake tins. Combine the dry ingredients in a bowl. Whisk the wet ingredients together in a jug. Sift half the flour mixture into a bowl and stir in half the buttermilk mixture. Sift and stir in the remaining flour mixture, then the remaining liquid. Divide the mixture between the cake tins.
2. Bake in a preheated oven, 180°C (350°F), Gas Mark 4, for 25–30 minutes or until risen and just firm to the touch. Transfer to a wire rack to cool.
3. Beat the butter in a bowl with the cream cheese until well combined. Add the vanilla extract and icing sugar and beat until smooth.
4. Transfer one of the cakes to a plate and cover its surface with a layer of the frosting. Place the other cake on top and cover the sides and top with the remaining frosting.

KING OF MY TART

SERVES 6 | PREP: 15mins | COOKING TIME: 15–20mins

No technical skills are necessary for this quick and easy tart, as it uses ready-made puff pastry and ingredients you've probably already got in your store cupboard. It can be rustled up quickly and eaten just as fast! Make sure you slice the apples to the same thickness each time so that they cook evenly. Serve to your favourite king or queen with cream or vanilla ice cream – it's the one you've been waiting for!

KING OF MY TART

★ INGREDIENTS ★

375g (12oz) pack chilled all-butter puff pastry

flour, for dusting

5 dessert apples, cored and cut into thin slices

juice of 1 lemon

50g (2oz) unsalted butter, diced

3 tablespoons caster sugar

4 tablespoons apricot jam

★ METHOD ★

1. Line a large baking sheet with nonstick baking paper. Roll out the pastry on to a lightly floured surface, trimming as necessary, to make a neat 35cm (14 inch) square.
2. Place on the baking sheet and turn over the edges of the pastry all the way round to make a slightly raised border. This will prevent the filling from running out.
3. Toss the apples in the lemon juice. Dot some of the butter over the base of the pastry and sprinkle with 1 tablespoon of the sugar.
4. Arrange the apples in neat rows on the pastry, then dot with the remaining butter and sprinkle over the remaining sugar.
5. Place in a preheated oven, 220°C (425°F), Gas Mark 7, for 15–20 minutes or until golden and crisp.
6. Warm the apricot jam in a small saucepan, then brush over the apples and pastry. Serve immediately.

THE BEST SUNDAE

SERVES 4 | PREP: 10mins

'The Best Day' appears on *Fearless*, which was written by Taylor when she was in her late teens. She wrote and recorded this song in secret as a Mother's Day gift for her mom, and even compiled a video of family footage showing the two of them through the years to accompany it. In honour of these kind of special moments, this sundae represents a trip back to the ice cream-based treats of childhood. Assemble each one with love and share with your Very Important People. Side order of nostalgia optional.

★ INGREDIENTS ★

8 tablespoons shop-bought Belgian chocolate sauce

100g (3½ oz) chocolate chip cookies, broken into small pieces

16 small scoops of vanilla ice cream

200g (7oz) pink and white marshmallows

2–3 tablespoons mini marshmallows, to decorate

chocolate wafer straws, to decorate

★ METHOD ★

1. Place the chocolate sauce in a saucepan over a low heat and warm through.
2. Meanwhile, place a handful of the biscuits in each of 4 tall sundae glasses. Add 2 scoops of vanilla ice cream to each glass. Add 2g (1oz) of the marshmallows to each sundae, then spoon 1 tablespoon of the warm chocolate sauce over each. Repeat the layers, finishing with the chocolate sauce.
3. Decorate with a few mini marshmallows and a chocolate wafer straw. Serve immediately and eat with a long spoon.

I KNEW YOU WERE TRUFFLES

MAKES 24 | PREP: 45mins, plus chilling

COOKING TIME: 8mins

Take a step back and get these awesome chocolate truffles in your sights! You can use almost any kind of dark liqueur to flavour these, so feel free to experiment with whisky, amaretto or bourbon. Divide the mixture into smaller batches to try out different alcohols – just remember to reduce the amount in proportion to the chocolate mixture. To avoid any trouble, a good non-alcoholic flavour alternative is vanilla extract (2 teaspoons).

★ FUN FACT ★

Taylor loves hot chocolate (with her chai cookies!) and a chocolate milkshake is her fast food beverage of choice.

I KNEW YOU WERE TRUFFLES

★ INGREDIENTS ★

250ml (8fl oz) double cream
200g (7oz) plain dark chocolate
3–4 tablespoons brandy or rum
2 tablespoons cocoa powder, sifted

TO DECORATE

200g (7oz) plain dark chocolate

★ METHOD ★

1. Pour the cream into a small pan and bring to the boil. Take the pan off the heat and break in 200g (7oz) plain dark chocolate. Leave to stand until it has melted, then stir in the brandy or rum and mix until smooth. Chill for 4 hours until the truffle mixture is firm.
2. Line a baking sheet with waxed paper and dust with cocoa powder. Scoop a little truffle mixture on to a teaspoon, then transfer it to a second spoon and back to the first again, making a well-rounded egg shape (or use a melon baller). Slide the truffle on to the cocoa-dusted paper. Once the mixture is used up, chill again for 2 hours, or overnight, until firm.
3. Melt 200g (7oz) plain dark chocolate in a bowl over a pan of simmering water. Stir well, then, holding 1 truffle at a time on a fork over the bowl, spoon melted chocolate over the top to coat it.
4. Place the truffles on a nonstick baking sheet. Swirl a little chocolate over the top of each with a spoon. Chill for at least 1 hour before eating.

SHAKE IT TOFFEE POPCORN

SERVES 4 | PREP: 5mins | COOKING TIME: 4mins

One mouthful of this freshly popped corn covered with a warm toffee and chocolate combo will stop the haters from hating! Just think, while you've been sticking with one traditional flavour all this time (sugar or salt, anyone?), you could have been getting down to this sweet treat!

SHAKE IT TOFFEE POPCORN

★ INGREDIENTS ★

50g (2oz) popping corn

250g (8oz) butter

250g (8oz) light muscovado sugar

2 tablespoons cocoa powder

★ METHOD ★

1. Microwave the popping corn in a large bowl with a lid on high (900 watts) for 4 minutes. Alternatively, cook in a pan with a lid on the hob, on a medium heat, for a few minutes until popping.
2. Meanwhile, gently heat the butter, muscovado sugar and cocoa powder in a pan until the sugar has dissolved and the butter has melted.
3. Stir the warm popcorn into the mixture and serve.

★ FUN FACT ★

Taylor performed 'Shake It Off' live on stage for the first time at the MTV Video Music Awards in 2014.

THE SMALLEST MANGO (SORBET) THAT EVER LIVED

SERVES 4 | PREP: 20mins, plus chilling

Once you've tried this sorbet, it will make all the others look like also-rans. It more than measures up in terms of flavour and texture, and there is no special equipment required. Lime is the perfect accompaniment to cut through the sweetness of the mango, and if you want to add a little extra crunch, serve with a sprinkle of toasted almonds or a light, vanilla shortbread cookie.

★ FUN FACT ★

Swifties have speculated over who Taylor was describing in the song, 'The Smallest Man Who Ever Lived', since it appeared on *The Tortured Poets Department*. Who do YOU think it is?

THE SMALLEST MANGO (SORBET) THAT EVER LIVED

★ INGREDIENTS ★

150g (5oz) caster sugar
250ml (8fl oz) lime juice
grated zest of 1 lime
3 mangoes, peeled and stoned
2 egg whites

★ METHOD ★

1. Line a 1kg (2lb) loaf tin with clingfilm or nonstick baking paper. Put the sugar in a saucepan, add 250ml (8 fl oz) water and warm gently until the sugar is dissolved. Remove from the heat and stir in the lime juice and grated zest.
2. Meanwhile, process the mango flesh to make a smooth purée, reserving four thin slices for the decoration. Stir the purée into the lime syrup and pour the mixture into the loaf tin. Freeze for at least 4 hours or overnight until solid.
3. Remove the sorbet from the tin and blend or process with the egg whites. Return the mixture to the tin and freeze until firm.
4. Before serving, decorate each portion of sorbet with a thin slice of mango.

★ FOOD SAFETY ★

As the flavour of fresh fruit sorbet deteriorates quickly, and this recipe also contains raw egg white, eat within 72 hours and discard any leftovers after this time.

EVERSM'ORES

MAKES 12 | PREP: 10mins

Over a century since a recipe for the 'Graham Cracker Sandwich' was printed, you'll find it reborn here as the 'Evers'more'. The name is a contraction of the words 'some more' as one really isn't enough, but no matter what it's called, it will always be a campfire staple! The marshmallows can be toasted over a gas flame, under a grill or over a firepit or BBQ, and any plain biscuit works as the 'bread' in this 'more-ish' delight. Enjoy this snack outdoors while recreating your own *Evermore* woodsy aesthetic!

EVERSM'ORES

★ INGREDIENTS ★

300g (10oz) milk or dark chocolate, broken into 12 pieces

24 digestive biscuits

24 marshmallows

★ METHOD ★

1. Flip 12 of the biscuits over on a plate or baking tray, and place a piece of chocolate on each one.
2. Toast two marshmallows on a skewer over a fire pit or barbecue. Once they are gooey or melted to your preferred consistency, put the marshmallow skewer onto each biscuit base and add another biscuit on top.
3. Grip the biscuits and carefully pull out the skewer to leave a chocolate and marshmallow sandwich.

OLD HABITS DIE ICE CREAMING

SERVES 4–6 | PREP: 15mins, plus freezing and setting

Fact: a bowl of ice cream is a simple yet effective way to de-stress after a break-up. Or you could, you know, write a song about the place where your boyfriend went without you when he forgot you could see his location on your phone. Old habits really do die screaming ...

★ FUN FACT ★

The Black Dog in Vauxhall, London is believed to be the bar that Taylor named this song after, leading to this city pub running a competition on Instagram – the first 100 people to come in and quote a lyric from the song got a free drink! They even reminded entrants to turn their location off before arrival!

Him

OLD HABITS DIE ICE CREAMING

★ INGREDIENTS ★

FOR THE ICE CREAM

500g (1lb) bananas
2 tablespoons lemon juice
3 tablespoons thick honey
150g (5oz) natural yogurt
100g (3½ oz) chopped nuts
150ml (¼ pint) double cream
2 egg whites

FOR THE PRALINE

50ml (2fl oz) water
170g (6oz) caster sugar
2 tablespoons golden syrup
175g (6oz) toasted almonds

★ METHOD ★

1. Put the bananas in a bowl with the lemon juice and mash until smooth. Stir in the honey, followed by the yogurt and nuts, and beat well. Whisk the cream until it forms soft swirls, then fold into the banana mix and freeze in a plastic container for 3–4 hours until partially frozen. (If you have an ice cream machine, follow the manufacturer's instructions for mixing the ingredients until half-frozen.)
2. Whisk the egg whites lightly until they form soft peaks. Add to the ice cream machine and continue to churn and freeze until completely frozen. Alternatively, break up the ice cream in the plastic container with a fork, then fold in the whisked egg white and freeze until firm.
3. Make the praline. Pour the measured water into a heavy saucepan and add the sugar and golden syrup. Simmer gently until the sugar has dissolved, then cook to a caramel-coloured syrup.
4. Place the toasted almonds on a lightly greased piece of foil and pour the syrup over. Leave to set for 1 hour. Once set, crush into small fragments and serve scattered over or mixed into the ice cream.

DRINKS

GETAWAY SIDECAR

SERVES 1 | PREP: 5mins

The Sidecar is a classic cocktail which became fashionable during the 1920s in the bars of Paris and London. As with all cocktails, the better the quality of the ingredients you use, the better the outcome. Anything less than the best might just turn this drink into a sideshow ...

GETAWAY SIDECAR

★ INGREDIENTS ★

50ml (2fl oz) VSOP Cognac or good quality brandy

25ml (1fl oz) Cointreau

15ml (½ fl oz) fresh lemon juice

1 tablespoon caster sugar

twist of orange peel, to decorate

★ METHOD ★

Optional: Prepare the cocktail glass by running the cut edge of a lemon around the rim of the glass. Dip the damp rim in a dish of caster sugar so that a thin crust is formed. Fill the glass with ice and chill the glass in the refrigerator for 30 minutes.

1. Combine the brandy, Cointreau and lemon juice in a cocktail shaker. Fill with ice.
2. Shake well for 10–15 seconds until chilled.
3. Strain into a cocktail glass.
4. Decorate with a twist of orange peel. To make: Wrap a thinly-peeled strip of orange rind around a metal straw or chopstick. Slide the twist off and lay it over the rim of the glass.

★ FUN FACT ★

The song 'Getaway Car' from *Reputation* (2017) references an 'Old Fashioned' cocktail, which is a mixture of bourbon, bitters and sugar.

BAD BLOODY MARY

SERVES 2 | PREP: 5mins

If you've got problems and don't think you can solve them, the Bloody Mary is the drink for you. It's relied upon by many as a brunch-time pick-me-up or hangover cure. No need to rub salt in the wound of any old feuds or lingering headaches, just let it season your drink, hey?

★ FUN FACT ★

The music video for 'Bad Blood' cost a cool $13 million dollars and featured members of Taylor's squad including Zendaya, Karlie Kloss, Mariska Hargitay, Jessica Alba, Selena Gomez, Ellen Pompeo and Lena Dunham.

BAD BLOODY MARY

★ INGREDIENTS ★

1 cup ice cubes
100ml (3½ fl oz) vodka
500ml (17fl oz) tomato juice
1 tablespoon fresh lemon juice
shake of Worcestershire sauce, to taste
shake of Tabasco sauce, to taste
celery salt, a pinch
black pepper, generous grind
2 celery sticks, to decorate
2 lemon slices, to decorate

★ METHOD ★

1. Place the ice in a large jug and pour over the vodka, tomato sauce and lemon juice.
2. Add the Worcestershire and Tabasco sauces, to taste, along with the celery salt and pepper.
3. Stir with a long metal spoon until the jug feels cold.
4. Strain into two tall glasses.
5. Decorate with the celery sticks and lemon, along with 3 extra ice cubes.

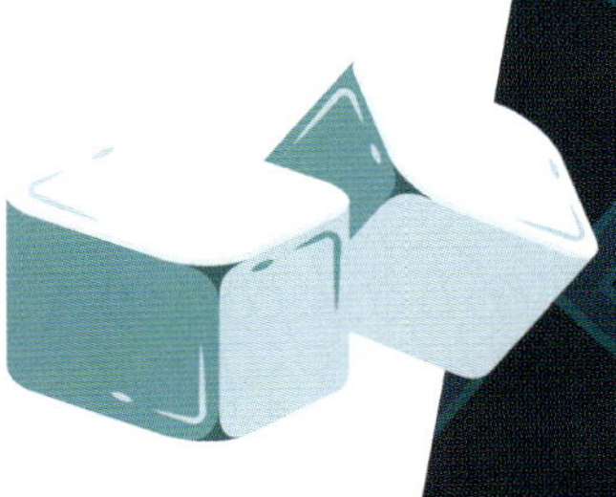

AFTERGLOW

SERVES 2 | PREP: 5mins

In the song, 'Afterglow', Taylor takes responsibility for an argument that got blown out of proportion and asks for forgiveness. Perhaps a make-up drink would help to cool the burn? This fruity mocktail emulates a 'sunrise' cocktail with its beautiful layers of red, orange and yellow. It will even let you show off your bartender skills thanks to some clever pouring. We'll meet you in the afterglow!

AFTERGLOW

★ INGREDIENTS ★

300ml (10fl oz) orange juice
1 cup ice cubes
grenadine
2 pineapple wedges, to decorate
2 maraschino cherries, to decorate
ice cubes

★ METHOD ★

1. Put the juices and ice into a cocktail shaker.
2. Shake for 10–15 seconds.
3. Pour the drink into two highball glasses.
4. Tilt each glass on an angle, taking care not to spill the drink, and gently pour the grenadine along the side. Allow it to sink to the bottom of the glass to create the sunset 'glow'.
5. Decorate with a wedge of pineapple and maraschino cherry, skewered together with a cocktail stick. Add 2–3 ice cubes and serve.

CHAMPAGNE PROBLEMS

SERVES 1 | PREP: 3mins

What's better than one Champagne cocktail recipe? That's right, THREE! Each of these Champagne-based drinks can also be made with sparkling wine, fizzy white grape juice or Prosecco, which should ensure there are no Champagne problems!

★ FUN FACT ★

Taylor was seen partying at the 2025 Grammys with a golden bottle of Armand de Brignac Blanc de Noirs No.4, which retails at over $300 per bottle.

★ MIMOSA ★

75ml (3fl oz) Champagne

75ml (3fl oz) fresh orange juice

orange slice, to decorate

1. Pour the Champagne into a chilled Champagne flute. Add the orange juice.
2. Decorate with a slice of orange (optional).

★ KIR ROYALE ★

1 tablespoon crème de cassis

150ml (5fl oz) Champagne

1 blackberry, to decorate

1. Pour the crème de cassis into the bottom of a Champagne flute. Top up the glass with the Champagne.
2. Drop in the blackberry to decorate.

★ CLASSIC FRENCH ★

1 cup ice cubes

25ml (1fl oz) gin

15ml (½ fl oz) simple syrup

15ml (½ fl oz) fresh lemon juice

75ml (3fl oz) Champagne

Lemon twist, to decorate

FOR THE SIMPLE SYRUP

100ml water

100g (2oz) granulated sugar

1. To make the simple syrup, combine the sugar and water in a small saucepan and allow to bubble gently over a medium heat until the sugar has dissolved.
2. Put the ice into the cocktail shaker. Pour over the gin, lemon juice and simple syrup. Shake for 10–15 seconds. Strain into a coupé glass and top with the Champagne. Decorate with a lemon twist (optional).

FLORIDA!!! FRUIT PUNCH

SERVES 6 | PREP: 5mins, plus chilling

Beat the heat with this zingy non-alcoholic fruit punch. The addition of ginger ale gives it both a lightly spiced kick and touch of fizz, but it works just as well without (or with lemonade).

FLORIDA!!! FRUIT PUNCH

★ INGREDIENTS ★

500ml (17fl oz) orange juice
500ml (17fl oz) cranberry juice
500ml (17fl oz) pineapple juice
juice of 2 limes
500ml (17fl oz) ginger ale
ice, to serve
6 strawberries, halved, to decorate
6 orange slices, to decorate

★ METHOD ★

1. Combine the orange, cranberry and pineapple juices in a large jug, along with the lime juice.
2. Refrigerate for 30–60 minutes to allow the flavours to blend.
3. Stir in the ginger ale and add the ice before serving.
4. Pour into glasses and decorate each one with two strawberry halves and a slice of orange.

★ FUN FACT ★

Florence Welch of Brit band Florence and the Machine features on the *Midnights* track 'Florida!!!' and performed the song with Taylor more than once on The Eras Tour. In 2015, Taylor said of her friend, "Every time I've been around her she is the most magnetic person in the room."

VALENTINE'S DAY VIRGIN COLADA

SERVES 4 | PREP: 5mins

This mocktail is the alcohol-free version of a traditional Piña Colada, which is a rum-based cocktail hailing from Puerto Rico. If you can't get coconut cream, chill a can of full-fat coconut milk and use the set cream from the top once the liquid separates.

VALENTINE'S DAY VIRGIN COLADA

★ INGREDIENTS ★

500ml pineapple juice
175ml (6fl oz) coconut cream
2–3 large cups of ice
pineapple wedges, to decorate
maraschino cherries, to decorate

★ METHOD ★

GO TAYLOR

1. Pour the pineapple juice and coconut cream into a jug blender.
2. Add ice to reach the maximum volume line.
3. Blend for 1–2 minutes until the mixture is smooth and no large pieces of ice remain.
4. Pour into glasses and decorate with the pineapple wedge and maraschino cherry.

★ FUN FACT ★

The 2010 movie, *Valentine's Day*, features the song 'Today Was a Fairytale', written and performed by Taylor, who also had a role in the film alongside then-boyfriend, Taylor Lautner.

LAVENDER HAZE LEMONADE

SERVES 4 | PREP: 5mins

When the lavender haze creeps up on you, a cooling glass of this lemonade will cool you down. If you can't get hold of ready-made lavender syrup, make your own by adding 2 teaspoons of culinary lavender* to the simple syrup recipe on page 127. Boil the water and then remove from the heat. Infuse the lavender buds in the water for 5–10 minutes. Add the sugar and return the pan to the heat so that it dissolves. Strain well before cooling.

LAVENDER HAZE LEMONADE

★ INGREDIENTS ★

250ml (8fl oz) lemon juice

1l (1¾ fl oz) water

100ml (3½ fl oz) lavender syrup

simple syrup, (optional, see recipe on page 127)

ice, to serve

lemon slices, to decorate

lavender stalks, to decorate

★ METHOD ★

1. Pour the lemon juice, water and lavender syrup into a tall jug.
2. Stir gently to combine.
3. Check the flavour – add some of the simple syrup if the lemonade isn't as sweet as you would like.
4. Pour into glass mugs or tall glasses, add ice and decorate with a lemon slice and lavender stalk.*

* Reminder: While some flowers are edible, only culinary lavender should be used for cooking and the lavender stalks should not be ingested.

MISS AMERICANA AMARETTO COFFEE

SERVES 1 | PREP: 5mins

A liqueur coffee makes a warming end to a perfect evening, especially when topped with indulgent cream and served with crispy amaretti biscuits. Use a good quality coffee and replace the Amaretto with Irish whiskey for an Irish coffee or Baileys liqueur if you prefer a creamier taste.

★ FUN FACT ★

In 2021, Starbucks renamed Taylor's favourite coffee order – their grande caramel non-fat latte – as 'Taylor's Latte' or 'Taylor's Version', to tie-in with the album release of *RED (Taylor's Version).*

MISS AMERICANA AMARETTO COFFEE

★ INGREDIENTS ★

25ml (1fl oz) Amaretto liqueur

200ml (7fl oz) strong black coffee

whipped cream

grated dark chocolate, to decorate

amaretti biscuits, to serve (optional)

★ METHOD ★

1. Pour the amaretto into a tall coffee glass.
2. Add the strong black coffee and stir to mix.
3. Top with whipped cream.
4. Decorate with the grated dark chocolate.
5. Serve with amaretto biscuits on the side.

SLOE LONG, LONDON

SERVES 2 | PREP: 5mins

A gin fizz is a classic cocktail recipe, and this one is made with sloe gin, which makes the cocktail sweeter than usual. If you don't have sloe gin, simply use regular gin and include the elderflower liqueur to achieve the sweetness and enhance the elderflower flavour.

SLOE LONG, LONDON

★ INGREDIENTS ★

50ml (2fl oz) sloe gin

25ml (1fl oz) elderflower liqueur (optional)

1 tablespoon elderflower cordial

25ml (1fl oz) lemon juice

75ml (3fl oz) sparkling wine

1 cup ice cubes

mint leaves, to decorate

★ METHOD ★

1. Pour the gin, elderflower liqueur (if using), elderflower cordial and lemon juice into a cocktail shaker.
2. Add the ice and shake well for around 30 seconds, or until the outside of the shaker is cold.
3. Strain into two coupé glasses.
4. Fill the glasses with the sparkling wine.
5. Decorate with a mint leaf and serve immediately.

★ FUN FACT ★

Much like Taylor, London and gin have a rich history. During London's Gin Craze in the 18th century around 10 million gallons of gin were being distilled in the capital per year, and London Dry remains a popular style of gin.

★ RECIPE NOTES ★

★ RECIPE NOTES ★

★ RECIPE NOTES ★

★ RECIPE NOTES ★

★ INDEX ★

(198)9 Bean and Herb Salad 76
Afterglow 124
ale 61
All Too Wellington 80
Amaretto liqueur 135
Antipasti Hero 48
apples, cooking 75
apples, dessert 23, 85, 105
Are You Bready For It? 30
artichokes 49

bacon 33, 67
Bad Bloody Mary 122
bananas 89, 117
Bangers and Nashville 84
beans, butter 77
beans, cannellini 77
beans, French 73
beans, green 77
beans, haricot 67
beef fillet 81
beer batter 51
Bejeweled Rice Pilaf 42
Better Than Revenge Spicy Jalapeños 52
Billboard Cheeseboard with Green Tomato Chutney 74
blueberries 17, 19, 21
Bombalurina Banoffee Pie 88
Brazil nuts 99
bread 11, 27, 31, 33, 83, 95
But Daddy I Love Hummus 54
buttermilk 103

cabbage, red 71
cabbage, white 37
cauliflower 65
Chai tea bags 99
Chai Teabread 98
Champagne 127
Champagne Problems 126
cheese, Brie 27, 75
cheese, cream 29, 53, 97, 103
cheese, halloumi 39
Cheese, mozzarella 49
Cheese, provolone 63
cherries 21
Cherry Lips Breakfast Smoothie 20
chickpeas 55
chicken, breasts 29, 73
chicken, wings 37
chipotle sauce 53
chocolate chip cookies 107
chocolate sauce 107
chocolate spread 13
Christmas Tree Farm Pastries 12
cinnamon sugar 15, 101
cocoa nibs 21
cocoa powder 103, 109, 111
coconut cream 131
coconut milk 65
coffee, black 135
Cointreau 121
coleslaw 37
condensed milk 88
Corn-elia Street Fritters 46
Cowboy Like Beans 66
creamed coconut 45
crème de cassis 127
crème fraîche 69
croissant dough 15
Cruel Summer Pudding 94

dark chocolate 89, 91, 93, 109, 115, 135
Deli-cate BLT Sandwich 32
digestive biscuits 89, 97, 115
double cream 89, 91, 93, 109, 117
Doughnut Blame Me 100
dried fruit 99

eggs 11, 17, 35, 79, 93, 97, 103
elderflower liqueur 137
Eversm'ores 114
Fearless Fish Tacos 70

fennel 83
fettuccini 59
figs 39
Filo-ing 22 Spinach and Filo Pie 34
fish, white 71
Florida!!!! Fruit Punch 128
Friendship Fries 40

Getaway Sidecar 120
gin 127
ginger ale 129
gravy 85
grenadine 125
Guilty as Cinnamon Rolls 14

ham 69
honey 19, 23, 37, 117

INDEX

I Can Do It With a Broken Tart 78
I Knew You Were Truffles 108
ice cream, vanilla 107
Illicit Eclairs 92

jalapeños 53, 71

ketchup 37, 41
King of My Tart 104

lager 51
lamb 43
Lavender Haze Lemonade 132
lavender syrup 133
lettuce 33
Look What You Made Me Fondue 90
Lover-micelli Soup 72

mango 113
'Marry Me' Juliet Fettucini 58
marshmallows 91, 107, 115
mascarpone cheese 59
Midnight Muffins 16
Mildest Dreams Vegetable Korma 64
Miss Americana Amaretto Coffee 134
muesli 23
mushrooms 61, 79, 81

nuts, cashew 21
nuts, pecan 15, 27
nuts, pine 35, 43

oats 19, 21
Old Habits Die Ice Creaming 116
olives 31, 39, 49, 77, 83
onions 43, 51, 53, 63, 75, 81, 85
Out of the Woods Bircher Muesli 22

Paper Onion Rings 50
pastry, filo 35
pastry, puff 13, 39, 81, 105
pastry, shortcrust 61, 79
peas 65, 69, 73
pepper, green 65
pepper, red 29, 31, 45, 65, 83
pepper, yellow 29
peppers, chargrilled 49
Philly Cheesesteak 62
pomegranate seeds 43
popping corn 111
potatoes 41, 85
potatoes, baking 65
potatoes, new 77
potatoes, sweet 45
praline 117
prosciutto 49

raspberries 95, 97
RED Velvet Cake 102
redcurrants 95
rice 43
rose harissa paste 55

salami 49
salsa 47
sausages 85
Shake It Toffee Popcorn 110
Shakshuka It Off 10
Shawarma is My Boyfriend 28
simple syrup 127
sloe gin 137
Sloe Long, London 136
Snake and Ale Pie 60
spinach 35, 59
steak 61, 63
Stew Romantics 82
strawberries 91, 95, 129
Sweet Nothing Potato Soup 44
sweetcorn 47

tahini 55
tartare sauce 71
The Best Sundae 106
The Smallest Mango (Sorbet) That Ever Lived 112
The Tortellini Poets Department 68
This is Why We Can't Have Nice Wings 36
Toler-oat It Granola 18
tomatoes 29, 31, 33, 47, 53, 65, 73, 83
tomato juice 123
tomato, cherry 11, 41, 45
tomato, sun-dried 49, 59
tortellini 69
tortillas 29, 71

Valentine's Day Virgin Colada 130
vermicelli 73
vodka 123
VSOP Cognac 121

Welcome to New York Cheesecakes 96
Who's Afraid of Little Old Halloumi? 38
wine, sparkling 137

yeast, dried 101
You Belong with Brie 26